THE
PARTY GIRLS

By Amy Rosenthal

The Party Girls was first performed at the Marlowe Theatre,
Canterbury, on 1 September 2025

THE
PARTY GIRLS

CAST
Nancy Mitford — **Kirsty Besterman**
Bob Treuhaft — **Joe Coen**
Diana Mitford — **Elisabeth Dermot Walsh**
Jessica 'Decca' Mitford — **Emma Noakes**
Unity Mitford — **Ell Potter**
Debo Mitford — **Flora Spencer-Longhurst**

PRODUCTION
Playwright — **Amy Rosenthal**
Director — **Richard Beecham**
Designer — **Simon Kenny**
Lighting Designer — **Aideen Malone**
Composer & Sound Designer — **Adrienne Quartly**
Video Designer — **Dick Straker**
Movement Director — **Quinny Sacks**
Fight Director — **Haruka Kuroda**
Casting Director — **Annelie Powell** CDG
Associate Director — **Millie Foy**
Props Supervisor — **Kelly Evans**
Costume Supervisors — **Laura Rushton / Melanie Brookes**
Wigs, Hair & Make-up Supervisor — **Kelly Cox**

CAST

Kirsty Besterman
Nancy Mitford

Theatre includes *Habeas Corpus* at the Menier Chocolate Factory; *Macbeth* for the National Theatre and on UK tour; *Genesis Inc.* and *Experience* at the Hampstead Theatre; *Winter Solstice* for Actors Touring Company; *Betrayal*, *Separate Tables*, and *Dangerous Corner* at Salisbury Playhouse; *They Drink It in the Congo* at the Almeida Theatre; *Tipping the Velvet* at the Lyric Hammersmith; *Arcadia* and *Tonight at 8.30* for English Touring Theatre; *Private Lives* at the Royal Lyceum; *The School for Scandal* at the Park Theatre; *Playhouse Creatures* at Chichester Festival Theatre; *Foxfinder* at the Finborough Theatre; *The Importance of Being Earnest* at the Rose Theatre, Kingston; *Edmond* and *The Great Gatsby* at Wilton's Music Hall; *Liberty*, *Much Ado About Nothing*, *The Merchant of Venice*, and *Holding Fire* at Shakespeare's Globe; *Twelfth Night* at Ludlow Theatre Festival; *Amy's View* at Nottingham Playhouse; *The Rivals* at Theatre Royal Bath; *Othello* for Cheek by Jowl; and *King Lear* for the RSC.

Television: *The Sandman*, *Vigil*, *Professor T*, *Grantchester*, *Top Boy*, *War of the Worlds*, *Doctor Who*, *His Dark Materials*, *Holby City*, *Father Brown*, *Silent Witness*, *Foyle's War*, and *Doctors*.

Film: *Rupture* and *Chicken*.

Joe Coen
Bob Treuhaft

Theatre includes *Leopoldstadt* and *Birdsong* in the West End; *The Sweet Science of Bruising* at Southwark Playhouse; *A Dark Night in Dalston* at the Park Theatre; *The Mighty Walzer* and *Edward II* at the Royal Exchange Theatre; *Bad Jews* in the West End and at the St. James' Theatre and the Ustinov Studio at Theatre Royal Bath; and *The Rubenstein Kiss* at Nottingham Playhouse and the Yvonne Arnaud.

Television: *Kaos*, *The Outlaws*, *Angela Black*, *Plebs*, *The Lost Honour of Christopher Jeffries*, *Da Vinci's Demons*, and *The Bible*.

Film: *The Critic*, *Son of God*, and *City Rats*.

Elisabeth Dermot Walsh
Diana Mitford

Theatre includes *Ring Round the Moon* and *The Country Wife* in the West End; *The Alchemist* and *The Life of Galileo* at the National Theatre; *Rebecca* on UK tour; *The Rivals* at Bristol Old Vic; *Aristocrats* at the Abbey Theatre; *The Misanthrope* and *The Shape of Things* at the Gate Theatre, Dublin; *Pride & Prejudice* and *Two Plays After: The Bear* for the Gate Theatre at the Spoleto Festival; *Cyrano de Bergerac* at Nuffield Southampton Theatres; *The Winslow Boy* and *Easy Virtue* at Chichester Festival Theatre; and *Wuthering Heights* at West Yorkshire Playhouse.

Television: *Miss Scarlet and The Duke*, *Sister Boniface Mysteries*, *Doctors*, *The Well*, *Holby City*, *Fiona's Story*, *Midsomer Murders*, *The Commander*, *Love Soup*, *Twenty Thousand Streets Under the Sky*, *Poirot*, *My Hero*, *Murphy's Law*, *Bertie and Elizabeth*, *Love in a Cold Climate*, *Cleopatra*, *Falling For A Dancer* and *Unfinished Business*.

Film: *From Time to Time*.

Emma Noakes
Jessica 'Decca' Mitford

Theatre includes *Rebus: A Game Called Malice* at Queen's Theatre, Hornchurch; *Abigail's Party* at the Park Theatre; *The Rover*, *Two Noble Kinsmen*, and *The Winter's Tale* for the RSC; *Separate Tables* and *Bedroom Farce* at Salisbury Playhouse; *Proof*, *The Rivals*, and *The Admirable Crichton* at the New Vic Theatre; *Charged* at Soho Theatre; *Wuthering Heights* at Birmingham Rep; *Pygmalion* at the Old Vic; and *The Sea* in the West End.

Television: *Casualty*, *Call the Midwife*, *The Salisbury Poisonings*, *Shakespeare and Hathaway*, *New Worlds*, *Doctors*, *Holby City*, and *The Bill*.

Film: *The Other Boleyn Girl*.

Radio includes *Mr. Pye*, *Road to Ferrera*, *Shakespeare's Fire*, *Mad Girl*, *The Fall and Rise of Danny Clarke*, *Maurice*, and *The Brothers Karamazov*.

Ell Potter
Unity Mitford

Theatre includes *The Last Show Before We Die*, *HOTTER*, and *FITTER* (also Ellie Keel Productions) for the HOTTER Project; and *Peter Pan* at Shipwright Theatre.

Television: *Cheaters* and *Doctor Who*.

Audiobooks include *Hamnet*, *Boy*, *To the Lighthouse*, *All Our Yesterdays*, *Something Extraordinary*, *Mary and the Birth of Frankenstein*, *Trouble*, *Under the Harrow*, *Berlin*, *Winter Dark*, *A Most Intriguing Lady*, *Marvellous*, *Tell Me How It Ends*, *Beyond That, the Sea*, *Emily Wilde's Encyclopaedia of English Fairies*, *Briefly, A Delicious Life*, *Elsewhere*, *Twin Crowns*, *Miss Eliza's English Kitchen*, *The Shape of Darkness*, and *The Great Godden*.

Radio includes *It's Me*, *Tess of the D'Urbervilles*, *The Girls of Slender Means*, *The Snow and the Works on the Northern Line*, *In at the Deep End*, *The Mill on the Floss*, *Dark, Salt, Clear*, *The Blackrock Girl*, *The Country Girls Trilogy*, and *The Unwelcome*.

Flora Spencer-Longhurst
Debo Mitford

Theatre includes *The Forsyte Saga* and *A Pupil* at the Park Theatre; *And Then There Were None* for Fiery Angel and on China tour; *Once*, *Girl With a Pearl Earring* and *Amélie* in the West End; *Seagulls* and *Beryl* at the Octagon Bolton; *The Real Thing* for the

Rose Theatre, Kingston, Theatre Royal Bath and Cambridge Arts Theatre; *Much Ado About Nothing*, *Love's Labour's Lost*, and *The Christmas Truce* for the RSC; *Titus Andronicus* at Shakespeare's Globe; *The Importance of Being Earnest – A New Musical* at Theatre Royal Windsor; *Wonderland* at Riverside Studios and the Assembly Rooms; *The Beggar's Opera* at Regent's Park Open Air Theatre; *A Christmas Carol* at King's Head Theatre; *Ghosts* and *The Member of the Wedding* at the Young Vic; and *The Children's Hour* at the Royal Exchange Theatre.

Television: *Waiting for the Out*, *Oasis*, *Midsomer Murders*, *The Bastard Executioner*, *Father Brown*, *Leonardo*, *Chickens*, *Unforgiven*, *Wallander*, *The Real Deal*, *Losing It*, *The Family Man*, *Lewis*, and *Dalziel & Pascoe*.

Film: *Say Your Prayers*, *Walking with the Enemy*, and *The Irish Connection*.

PRODUCTION

Amy Rosenthal
Playwright

Theatre includes *Birth* (at Soho Theatre) and *A Quiet Voice* (at the Kiln Theatre) for Emanate Productions; *Fear of Cherry Blossom* at the Everyman Theatre Studio; *Pelican Daughters* at the Shakespeare in Shoreditch Festival/RIFT; *Entanglement* (libretto) for Nova Music Opera and on UK tour; *Polar Bears* for A Play, A Pie and A Pint at West Yorkshire Playhouse; *The Tailor Made Man* (book) in the West End; *Beware Young Girls* (co-written with Kate Dimbleby) at the Crazy Coqs; *The Man Who Came to Brunch* for the Bush Theatre and Sixty-Six Books; *Liberation* for Yad Arts and the Tricycle Theatre; *Jitterbug Blitz* for the Lyric Hammersmith Young Company; *On the Rocks* at the Hampstead Theatre; *Sitting Pretty* at Watford Palace Theatre, on UK tour and at Hypothetical Theatre, New York; *Henna Night* at the Scarborough Festival and Chelsea Theatre; *Jerusalem Syndrome* at the Royal Exchange Theatre and Soho Theatre; and *Lifelines* for the Royal Court Young Writers Festival.

Radio includes, for BBC Radio 4, *Thin Ice* and *Little Words*; and *Cold Enough for Snow*, *Eskimo Day*, *Bar Mitzvah Boy*, *Tortoise*, and *Jack Rosenthal's Last Act*, adapted from the work of Jack Rosenthal.

Film: *The Clinic* (in development) and *That Woman* (UK Jewish Film Festival, Pears Short Film winner).

Richard Beecham
Director

Training: University of Oxford, RADA/King's College London, and National Theatre Studio.

Theatre includes *Duet for One* at the Orange Tree Theatre; *Footfalls/Rockaby* (also Jermyn Street Theatre), *Driving Miss Daisy* (also UK tour), *In a Garden*, *Red Light Winter*, and *Henry IV, Part 1* at Theatre Royal Bath; *Gaslight*, *Broken Glass*, *How the Other Half Loves*, *Neville's Island*,

and *A Taste of Honey* at Watford Palace Theatre; *84 Charing Cross Road* at Cambridge Arts Theatre and on UK tour; *Rose* at HOME Manchester; *Playing for Time* at the Crucible Theatre, Sheffield; *Dancing at Lughnasa*, *In Praise of Love*, and *Humble Boy* at the Royal Theatre, Northampton,; *Rutherford & Son* at Northern Stage; *The Human Cost* and *Just Before the War* at the Young Vic; *The School for Scandal*, *The Invention of Love*, *Side by Side by Sondheim*, and *The Miser* at Salisbury Playhouse; *Charley's Aunt*, *Private Lives*, *Two Gentlemen of Verona*, and *Black Comedy/Real Inspector Hound* at Exeter Northcott Theatre; *Romeo & Juliet* for Creation Theatre Company, Oxford; *The Bench* at Battersea Arts Centre; *Early One Morning* and *Entertaining Mr Sloane* at Octagon Bolton; and *Eulogy for a Hard Man* at Live Theatre, Newcastle.

Film includes *The Guitar*.

Simon Kenny
Designer

Theatre includes *A Thousand Splendid Suns* at Birmingham Rep; *The Lord Of The Rings: A Musical Tale* (also Chicago, Australia and New Zealand), *Whistle Down The Wind*, *Assassins* (also Nottingham Playhouse), *Sleeping Beauty*, *The Ladykillers*, and *Sleuth* at the Watermill Theatre; *Rehab the Musical*, *Sweeney Todd* (also off-Broadway), and *The Selfish Giant* in the West End; *The Lion* at Southwark Playhouse (also Arizona Theatre Company, Japan and South Korea); *The Wiz* at Hope Mill Theatre; *Saturday Night Fever* (also UK tour), *In the Next Room or the vibrator play*, and *4000 Miles* at Theatre Royal Bath; *The Unseen* at Riverside Studios; *Here in America* and *Duet for One* at the Orange Tree Theatre; *Steel* and *Brassed Off* at Theatre by the Lake; *Murder in the Dark* on UK tour; *Blue/Orange* at Royal & Derngate Northampton; *The Art of Illusion* and *The Death of a Black Man* at the Hampstead Theatre; *Footfalls/Rockaby* at Jermyn Street Theatre; and *Giraffes Can't Dance* at the Curve Theatre, Leicester.

Dance and opera include *Link in My Bio* at Luxembourg Opera; *Our Mighty Groove* at Sadler's Wells East; *A Midsummer Night's Dream* and *Le Nozze di Figaro* at Nevill Holt Opera; and *Vivienne* at the Royal Opera House.

Aideen Malone
Lighting Designer

Theatre includes *Kyoto* for the RSC; *Twelfth Night*, *Carousel*, and *Fiddler on the Roof* (also Barbican; Olivier nomination for Best Lighting Design) at Regent's Park Open Air Theatre; *Dracula: Mina's Reckoning* for the National Theatre of Scotland (Profile Award honourable mention); *Lemons Lemons Lemons Lemons Lemons* and *Hetty Feather* in the West End; *Wonder Boy*, *You Bury Me*, and *A Monster Calls* (also Old Vic) at Bristol Old Vic; *Duet for One* at the Orange Tree Theatre; *The Clothes They Stood Up In* at Nottingham Playhouse; *Running With Lions* at the Lyric

Hammersmith; *Hamlet* and *Death of a Salesman* (also West End; Knights of Illumination nomination) at the Young Vic; *Old Bridge* at the Bush Theatre; *A Kind Of People* at the Royal Court Theatre; *Brighton Rock* at York Theatre Royal; *La Strada* at the Other Palace; and *Jane Eyre* and *Peter Pan* at the National Theatre.

Adrienne Quartly
Composer & Sound Designer

Theatre, as composer, includes *The Tempest* for the RSC; *Gunpowder Plot Immersive Experience* at the Tower of London; *The Two of Us* at Watford Palace Theatre; *Kim's Convenience* on UK tour; and *Queen Margaret* at the Royal Exchange Theatre. As sound designer: *The Cat and the Canary* at Chichester Festival Theatre; *Get Happy* at the Barbican; *The Nutcracker* at Bristol Old Vic; *Bad Jews* in the West End; *Splendour* at the Donmar Warehouse; *A Tale of Two Cities* on UK tour; *Citysong* at the Abbey Theatre and Soho Theatre; *Opening Skinner's Box/The Paper Man* for Improbable; *Cuttin' It* at the Young Vic; *Black Men Walking* for the Royal Court Theatre and Eclipse Theatre Company; *Rose* at HOME Manchester; and *Playboy of the Western World* at the National Theatre.

Film includes, as composer, *7 Deadly Idiots* for Told by an Idiot.

Audio includes, as sound designer, *Mansfield Park* for Audible.

Dick Straker
Video Designer

Theatre includes *Liberation* at the Royal Exchange Theatre; *The Borrowers*, *Walls and Windows*, and *Tales of Ballycumber* at the Gate Theatre, Dublin; *A Monster Calls* (also Bristol Old Vic) and *Richard II* at the Old Vic; *Peter Gynt* (also Edinburgh Festival Fringe), *Jumpers*, *Henry V*, *The Powerbook*, and *The Coast of Utopia* at the National Theatre; *Don Juan in Soho*, *The Mountaintop*, and *The Woman in White* (also Broadway) in the West End; *Cymbeline* and *Love's Sacrifice* for the RSC; *Roots* at the Donmar Warehouse; *Going Dark* for Fuel Theatre and the Young Vic; *Orpheus* at the Old Vic Tunnels; *Tiger Country* at the Hampstead Theatre; *Seize the Day* at the Tricycle Theatre; *Sugar Mummies* and *Hitchcock Blonde* at the Royal Court Theatre; *Julius Caesar* at the Barbican and on UK tour; and *Riverdance* at the Point Theatre, Dublin.

Opera includes *La Bohème* at Malmö Opera; *The Force of Destiny* at Greek National Opera; *Rusalka* at the Opéra Royal de Wallonie-Liège; *Aida* and *Andrea Chenier* at Opera North; *Greek* for Scottish Opera; *Notorious* at Göteborg Opera; and *The Ring Cycle* for the Royal Opera House.

Quinny Sacks
Movement Director

As a dancer, Quinny performed with Rambert Dance Company, Tanz Forum Köln and the Bejart Ballet.

As choreographer and movement director, theatre includes *Much Ado About Nothing* at Cambridge Arts Theatre; *Driving Miss Daisy* at Theatre Royal Bath; *Waste*, *Lady in the Dark*, and *Machinal* at the National Theatre; *Mojo*, *Mouth to Mouth*, and *Lights* at the Royal Court Theatre; *A Doll's House* at the Young Vic (also West End and New York); *Nijinsky* at Chichester Festival Theatre; *The Comedy of Errors* at Regent's Park Open Air Theatre; *A Winter's Tale*, *Les Enfants du Paradis*, and *Hamlet* for the RSC; *Private Lives* in the West End and on Broadway; *The Threepenny Opera* at the Donmar Warehouse; and *My Fair Lady*, *Summer Holiday*, and *The Boyfriend* on UK tour.

Opera includes *Lady Macbeth of Mtensk and The Fairy Queen* for English National Opera; and *The Voyage* at the Metropolitan Opera.

Film includes *Who Framed Roger Rabbit*, *Operation Mincemeat*, *Captain America*, *Troy*, *Johnny English*, *Captain Corelli's Mandolin*, *Shakespeare in Love*, *The Importance of Being Earnest*, *The Visitors*, *RKO 281*, *Dido and Aeneas*, and *Restoration*.

Television includes *The Singing Detective*, *Lipstick on Your Collar*, *Out of Her Mind*, *Catherine the Great*, *Keen Eddie*, *The Last of the Blond Bombshells*, and *Sex, Chips and Rock 'n' Roll*.

Haruka Kuroda
Fight Director

Theatre includes, as intimacy and fight director: *Rodelinda* at Garsington Opera; *This Bitter Earth* at Soho Theatre; *Noises Off* at New Wolsey Theatre; *The House Party* at Leeds Playhouse and on UK tour; *Three Sisters*, *The Taming of the Shrew*, and *Ghosts* at Shakespeare's Globe; *A Raisin in the Sun* for Headlong, Leeds Playhouse, Oxford Playhouse and the Lyric Hammersmith; *La Traviata* for English National Opera; *Underdog: The Other Other Brontë* at the National Theatre; *untitled f*ck m*ss s*igon play* at the Royal Exchange Theatre; and *Miss Saigon the Musical* and *The Crucible* at Sheffield Crucible.

As intimacy director: *Burlesque the Musical* in the West End; *Henry VIII* at Guildhall School of Music & Drama; and *The Voice of the Turtle* at Jermyn Street Theatre.

As fight director: *Of Mice And Men* at Derby Theatre; *Kinky Boots* at Curve Theatre, Leicester; *Ballet Shoes* at the National Theatre; and *Never Let Me Go* at the Rose Theatre, Kingston.

Television, as intimacy coordinator: *Beyond Paradise*, *Mandrake*, *Strike*, *Boarders*, *Such Brave Girls*, *Protection*, *Rivals*, *Silent Witness*, *Real Friend*, *History of a Pleasure Seeker*, *Culprits*, *Sherwood*, *Shogun*, *Superhoe*, and *Life After Life*.

Film, as intimacy coordinator: *Mother's Pride*, *Marriage Unplugged*, and *Re-Live*.

Annelie Powell CDG
Casting Director

Annelie is Creative Associate at Jonathan Church Theatre

Productions and a freelance casting director. She was previously Head of Casting at Nuffield Southampton Theatres, and prior to that she spent five years at the RSC.

Theatre includes *Wendy & Peter Pan* for the RSC; *Treasure Island* and *Wonder Boy* (also UK tour) at Bristol Old Vic; *Poor Clare* and *Playhouse Creatures* at the Orange Tree Theatre; *The Enormous Crocodile* at Regent's Park Open Air Theatre and on UK tour; *Apex Predator* at the Hampstead Theatre; *Kathy & Stella Solve a Murder!* in the West End; *Now That's What I Call a Musical!* on UK tour; *The Promise* and *Coram Boy* at Chichester Festival Theatre; *Taste of Honey* at the Royal Exchange Theatre; *In Dreams* at Leeds Playhouse; and *House of Shades* at the Almeida Theatre.

Millie Foy
Associate Director

Theatre, as director: *Like a Rat* at Camden People's Theatre; *Christbride* and *Screen Test* at the Edinburgh Festival Fringe; *Jinkies* at Camden Comedy Club; and *Four Go Off on One!* at Gilded Balloon.

As assistant director: *The Lion, the Witch & the Wardrobe* at Birmingham Rep; *Alice in Wonderland*, *Top Girls*, *Red Riding Hood*, and *Dogs* at Liverpool Everyman & Playhouse Theatres; *Romeo and Juliet* at Redgrave Theatre; and *Jeannie* at Finborough Theatre.

MARLOWE THEATRE

Marlowe Theatre Productions was set up in March 2025 as a trading company of the Marlowe Theatre Trust to develop and produce high-quality touring theatre, made in Kent.

All our productions originate at the Marlowe Theatre, Canterbury and benefit from opening in the theatre's 1200-seater main house or 150-seater studio. New productions can draw on our in-house expertise in producing, in programming and presenting touring work at scale, in technical, finance, learning and participation, marketing and comms.

Our Writers' Room, headed by Senior Producer Millie Brierley and Dramaturg Leo Butler, gives projects the time and support they need to develop. It is also a hub for new work in our region, offering writing programmes, nurturing new voices from Kent and creating an annual festival of new writing and industry insights.

Our ambition is to produce plays that speak to our times and to provide mainstream audiences across the UK with high-quality drama. We believe that new writing should be on our main stages and not just in studio theatres. We champion diversity and follow best practice in sustainable theatre-making.

The Party Girls by Amy Rosenthal is our first large-scale national touring production. This world premiere of a new play opens at the Marlowe Theatre in Canterbury on 1st September 2025.

THE PARTY GIRLS

Amy Rosenthal

Acknowledgements

The Party Girls has had quite a journey from page to stage, and I'm beyond grateful to everyone who supported it and brought it to life. Heartfelt thanks to John Terry of Chipping Norton Theatre and Rebecca Mordan of Scary Little Girls theatre company, who first drew me in to the world of the Mitfords; to Deborah Shaw, Millie Brierley, Leo Butler and everyone at the Marlowe Theatre, who met the play with passion and conviction and made it happen; to the actors who gave their time and talent to workshop it, notably Pippa Nixon, Claire Price and Tara Fitzgerald. To Deborah Halsey and all at Nick Hern Books for publishing this playtext; and to my dynamite agent Mel Kenyon, whose loyalty and laser insight I'll never take for granted. To our clever, committed creative team, not least our magnificent cast: Emma Noakes, Elisabeth Dermot Walsh, Kirsty Besterman, Ell Potter, Flora Spencer-Longhurst and Joe Coen, who have brought more to my words than I could ever have hoped; to inspired designer Simon Kenny and to my dream director Richard Beecham, who I must now persuade to work with me forever. To my playwright chums who've championed the play, and me, in particular Mark Rosenblatt, Ella Hickson, and the matchless *mensch* Phil Porter; to *all* my female friends, whose symbiotic camaraderie has given me a template for what it means to have sisters; and to my pals Nick Caldecott, Jerry Kenber and Jose Villoldo, true Hons. To my family; the Rosenthals, Galises and Turners, with special mention to my brilliant brother Adam and sister-in-law Taina; and to my mum, my heroine, Maureen Lipman, who I've been watching from the wings since birth (mine, not hers), and from whom I've learned everything about how and why I want to write.

This play is dedicated to Ava and Sacha Rosenthal, my niece and nephew, because it is the first play of mine that you will ever see, and I hope it makes you even half as proud as I am of you.

You do not have to be good
You do not have to walk on your knees
For a hundred miles through the desert, repenting,
You only have to let the soft animal of your body
Love what it loves

from 'Wild Geese' by Mary Oliver

Characters

BOB TREUHAFT, *American*
JESSICA MITFORD, *British, also known as* DECCA (*and by* UNITY, *as* BOUD)
NANCY MITFORD, *British, also known as* NAUNCE
DIANA MITFORD, *British, also known as* HONKS
UNITY MITFORD, *British, also known as* BOUD, *by* JESSICA
DEBORAH MITFORD, *British, known as* DEBO

The action of the play runs between the 1930s, 1940s and 1969, and between England, the USA and France, and very briefly, Germany. The characters age accordingly.

Mitford Words and Pronunciations

Hon – an honourable person; pronounced with a hard H, as in 'hen'
Counter-hon – the opposite; pronounced as above
Extrorder – extraordinary
Wondair – wonderful; pronounced 'wundare'
Muv – Mother
Farve – Father
On speakers – speaking to
Hilaire – hilarious
In pig – pregnant
Strongling – strong
Lumpular – lump

Notes on the Text

A 'beat' is no longer than a heartbeat, a musical beat rather than a pause.

A dash (−) indicates an interruption; feel free to fully interrupt and overlap, especially amongst the sisters. If a speech is broken by interruptions, the speaker should try to push on regardless, unless otherwise indicated.

This text went to press before the end of rehearsals and so may differ slightly from the play as performed.

ACT ONE

Scene One

September 1942, Washington DC.

It is early evening, not yet dark. JESSICA (*twenty-five*) *and* BOB (*thirty*) *stand by a fire escape outside the fashionable Troika nightclub.* JESSICA*'s manner is brisk, superficially friendly but firm.* BOB *squints at her, shiftily.*

JESSICA. Business or pleasure?

BOB. Huh?

JESSICA. Is that your car?

BOB. Why? Want a ride?

JESSICA. Did you drive here tonight for business or pleasure?

BOB. Say, that depends.

JESSICA. Shall we assume pleasure?

BOB. You bet, baby!

JESSICA. In that case, *sir,* you're in violation of the Ban on Pleasure Driving. According to which, as I'm sure you're aware, no gasoline ration may be used for the purposes of attending places of amusement –

BOB. Yeah, yeah –

JESSICA. Recreation or entertainment, such as theatres, concerts, dance halls –

BOB. Okay, lady –

JESSICA. Skating rinks, bowling alleys or *nightclubs.* You're squandering fuel at a time of international need and hampering your country's contribution to the war effort. We have a marvellous streetcar service in DC; I suggest you use it. (*Taking out her ID badge.*) I'm here on behalf on the OPA –

BOB. Behalf of-the-hell-what?

JESSICA. The *federal Office of Price Adminstration*, sir, to request that you hand over your ration book.

BOB. My –

JESSICA. Ration book, you heard me. Now.

She holds out her hand expectantly. BOB *bursts into delighted laughter.*

BOB. Terrific, Mrs Romilly! You got the job!

JESSICA. I thought I *had* the job.

BOB. You can have mine too; I'm keeping *schtum.*

JESSICA. Keeping what?

BOB. You're in charge! Your accent, your moxie –

JESSICA. Please, Mr Treuhaft, translate as you go!

BOB. Spirit, Mrs Romilly! *Moxie.* You are – dauntless. Those pleasure drivers will be quaking in their dance shoes.

JESSICA. I hope they're not all as seedy as *him*.

BOB. That's where I come in. Not that you need me. But if you did –

JESSICA. What would you do?

BOB *steps into the shadows and out again, gumshoe-style.*

BOB. 'Hold it there, mister, unless you want to see what a short-sighted Jew can do with a flask of joe and a slab of Hungarian cake.'

He slams down his briefcase on the fire escape and produces, with a flourish, a flask of coffee and two slabs of cake. JESSICA *watches, intrigued, as he decants the little picnic.*

JESSICA. Golly. None of the other lawyers provide cake.

ACT ONE, SCENE ONE

BOB (*mock-hurt*). You do this for *all* the lawyers?

JESSICA. Usually only in daylight.

BOB. Well, the others are regular guys, see? Home by six, pot-roast with the wife and kids, head hits the pillow and bang, they're on a tropical island with Betty Grable.

JESSICA. And you? Not a fan of Miss Grable?

BOB. Me, I'm grinding my teeth all night, wondering if the pleasure drivers of DC are complying with my little edict. It's my nature, Mrs Romilly. I can't give up.

JESSICA. Mr Treuhaft – did *you* draft the Pleasure Driving Ban?

BOB (*wry*). Hippest guy at the party, right?

JESSICA. Why, I think it's a splendid idea! You're saving gallons and gallons of petrol! You're fuelling tanks and fighter jets and submarines – and providing crucial support to the Allies! Besides, there are other forms of pleasure – (*Flushing.*) I mean –

BOB. Cake. For instance.

JESSICA. Cake!

He hands her a slice of cake in a napkin; she accepts it gratefully. Perches on the fire escape to eat it. Considers for a moment, then:

As it happens, it's my birthday.

BOB. Your birthday? Why aren't you out on the town?

JESSICA. I am, aren't I?

BOB. In a lousy car park?

JESSICA. I heard the Troika was the ultimate nightspot.

BOB. Sure, inside! You should've said.

JESSICA. Oh, I'm not wild about birthdays at the best of times, and twenty-five feels awfully dull and middle-aged.

BOB. Twenty-five? You're a spring lamb!

JESSICA. Baaaa.

BOB. Well, happy birthday. You're a sport to spend it like this.

JESSICA. It's a pleasure. I like to be busy.

She tucks into her cake. He observes her, enjoying her enjoyment.

This is scrummy, what is it?

BOB. *Rigó jancsi.* A Hungarian classic. Chocolate sponge, chocolate cream, apricot jam and a chocolate glaze. Jam's a little liquid, sorry –

JESSICA. Did you bake this?

BOB. I could lie.

JESSICA. It's home-made, I can tell.

BOB. Okay, cards on the table. Once a month, my mother sends me *rigó jancsi* from New York – sometimes still warm. My roommate waits by the door like a dog. You must know Ike, he's in Legal with me.

JESSICA. All the girls know Ike.

BOB. Know to avoid him, you mean.

JESSICA. Is he a particular chum?

BOB. He used to room with Joyce, his girl, but she got wise and went back to Ohio. I was looking for a place, so…

She raises her eyebrows, challenging. He laughs.

Listen, I don't approve of the way he carries on, but we rub along okay. I like his Duke Ellington records; he likes my mom's *heimishe* cake.

JESSICA. Translate?

BOB. Sorry, homely, from the homeland –

JESSICA. Is your mother from –

ACT ONE, SCENE ONE   11

BOB. Hungary. Or you might say Czechoslovakia. A tiny village, barely that. A handful of neighbours who upped and fled when trouble came and fetched up in the Bronx, including both my parents.

JESSICA (*caught by this*). They fled together?

BOB. Childhood sweethearts. She gets a job in a sweatshop, he waits tables. When they're old enough, they get hitched, and my sister and I grow up in the ghetto with our bitter old grandparents who refuse to speak a word of English till the day they die. But my mother, she has –

JESSICA. Moxie!

BOB. *Moxie.* She *works,* pushes, elbows her way into every room she needs to be in to scrape a living. And pushed my dad too, every day of his life – 'Be as good as you *are.* Be better!' Today, what can I tell you? She has her own hat shop on Park Avenue –

JESSICA (*bursting out*). She sounds a tremendous *Hon*!

BOB. A what?

JESSICA. Oh, it's what my sisters and I used to say if we approved of a person. A 'Hon' is a good egg, someone worth knowing – and a 'Counter-Hon' is the opposite, a rotter. Tell me more about your mother.

BOB. No, it's your turn.

JESSICA. Me? There's nothing to tell.

BOB. How old's your kid?

JESSICA. Eighteen months.

BOB. Got a snap?

She produces a picture from her purse, hands it over.

She's a peach. What's her name?

JESSICA. Constancia, she's called Constancia, but – this is rather silly –

BOB. Tell me.

JESSICA. We got into the habit of calling her Dinky before she was born. I was at the Democratic Convention in 1940 and I had frightful morning sickness – and someone said the baby must be kicking like the Democratic Donkey. Well, somehow it stuck, and we've called her Dinkydonk or Dink or the Donk ever since.

BOB. I *love* it! I was there in 1940. You see Mrs Roosevelt?

JESSICA. Wasn't she magnificent?

BOB. Wasn't she just!

JESSICA. Morning sickness be damned, I had to see her. There was even a gallant Texan who offered to let me throw up in his hat.

BOB. You take him up on it?

JESSICA. Fortunately the Dink held off and I didn't have to.

BOB. And does she still kick, now she's free?

JESSICA. Oh, Dinky's no trouble at all. Laughs at all my jokes and makes friends wherever we go.

BOB. She must be a hell of a comfort to you.

JESSICA (*sharp*). Comfort?

A beat.

BOB. I – mean to say, it can't be easy, that's all, on your own.

A chill has descended. Silence, broken by the purr of an approaching vehicle.

Here goes! If that's not a Pleasure Driver, I'll be –

The car veers off elsewhere with a screech of tyres. Silence again. JESSICA *shivers.*

You're cold.

JESSICA. I'm all right.

ACT ONE, SCENE ONE   13

BOB. Take my coat.

JESSICA. I'm fine, truly. I was raised in a series of enormous freezing country houses where one had to crouch in the airing cupboard and cling to the pipes for dear life.

BOB. Crouch in what?

JESSICA. The airing cupboard. A sort of closet where one keeps the immersion heater. Honestly, I'm used to the cold.

He lightly drapes his coat over her shoulders. A beat.

Thank you.

She pulls it tighter. Silence, then BOB *can take it no more.*

BOB. I feel terrible. I shouldn't have said –

JESSICA. It's my fault. I oughtn't to be so spiky.

BOB. It was insensitive of me.

JESSICA. I'm aware of the water-cooler gossip. (*American accent.*) 'Poor Decca Romilly, awful young to be a widow. Seems kind of queer she don't wear black.' (*She drops the accent.*) And I find it absurd. Thousands of men are missing in action, it's barely been a year. Yes, the official line is 'presumed *dead*' – but one can't presume anything, can one? My husband would *loathe* me to wear black and he hasn't the least intention of being killed. He's violently opposed to it – dying, that is. And Esmond doesn't do things he doesn't want to do.

BOB. Esmond must be quite a Hon.

JESSICA. I think you'd get on famously.

BOB. I think we *will.*

She smiles.

So the rest of your family's still in England, in the airing cupboard?

JESSICA. Oh, I haven't any family, not really.

BOB. I thought you said your sisters –

JESSICA. No, I haven't any sisters. It's just Dinky and Esmond and me.

Scene Two

Ten years earlier, September 1932. The schoolroom, Swinbrook House, England.

The room is cleanly divided in two, one side littered with German flags, posters and Fascist ephemera, the other with their Communist equivalents, including a plaster bust of Lenin.

UNITY (*eighteen*) *stands in the centre of the room, arms extended to the sides, wearing an ill-fitting ball-dress. There is a large, elderly white rat asleep on her shoulder.* DIANA (*twenty-two*), *her mouth full of pins, is artfully draping fabric around her.* NANCY (*twenty-eight*) *hovers impatiently.*

DIANA (*to* UNITY). Deep breath, darling.

UNITY *takes in a vast, exaggerated gulp of air.*

Weeny bit more if you can.

UNITY. I shall die.

NANCY (*to* DIANA). So shall I, Honks, if you make me wait any longer. I haven't all day.

DIANA. Go on then, I'm listening.

UNITY (*to* NANCY). What else have you to do?

NANCY. Finish my novel, sell it and make a fortune. You? (*To* DIANA.) Besides, the infants will appear any minute and we don't want *them* involved. Debo will have hysterics and as for Decca –

UNITY (*defensive*). What about Decca?

ACT ONE, SCENE TWO   15

NANCY. God only knows what Decca will do.

UNITY. They'll find out eventually.

DIANA. Keep still, angel. (*To* NANCY, *kindly.*) I said I'm listening.

NANCY *takes a deep breath.*

NANCY. All right. I'm speaking as the eldest sib, but everything I'm about to say is on behalf of Tom and Pamela as well. Tom and Pam feel exactly as I do, and if they were here, they'd back me up. In our collective view –

UNITY. 'In our collective view'! You sound like the Swinbrook vicar!

DIANA (*to* UNITY). Hush, and stop wriggling, or I shall pin *you.*

NANCY (*to* DIANA). Honks, can't we talk in private?

DIANA. Sorry, darling, has to be done. Muv said the dressmaker flatly refused to come back.

UNITY (*petting her rat*). Because she's scared of Ratular! The dressmaker, I mean. *Muv* isn't scared of anything, after the horror of spawning *us.*

DIANA. You *didn't* have Ratular at your fitting!

NANCY. Could we get back to the point?

UNITY. Had to try him with the frock, didn't I?

DIANA. Darling, you're the Honourable Unity Mitford, you'll be in *The Tatler*! You can't be presented to the King with a rat on your shoulder!

UNITY (*genuine*). Why?

DIANA. What if he scrams down your arm?

UNITY. He's too ancient to scram, he's barely alive.

NANCY (*to* DIANA). He could drop off and die in the Queen's *décolletage* and it wouldn't make half the stink of what you're proposing to do.

DIANA. I wish you wouldn't worry so.

NANCY. It's not just me, I told you. The siblings unite.

UNITY. Not I!

NANCY. The *grown-up* siblings. Tom and Pamela and I.

UNITY. I'm eighteen years old! I'm practically out! If I must endure this charade and wear this glorified nightgown in public then I'm entitled to declare my support for my darling Diana, even if you won't!

DIANA. Thank you, angel.

NANCY. We all *support* you – but we think you've gone mad. One *does* go mad. Shakespeare was right. A fairy dust has been sprinkled into your eyes and you've fallen in love with the very first creature –

UNITY. He's hardly an ass! He's the most exciting man in British politics! I think it's the most thrillingly romantic thing I've ever heard.

NANCY. It isn't *real.* What's real is her life with Bryan and the babies.

UNITY. What's real about that? It's all diamonds and houses and show!

NANCY. You don't know anything. Bryan adores her.

UNITY. She doesn't adore *him.* Bryan isn't sexy, is he, Honks?

DIANA *has drifted away, collecting up pearls and ostrich feathers, which she now starts adding to* UNITY*'s costume. She's humming to herself, remote, calm and happy.*

Honks?

DIANA. What, darling?

UNITY. Bryan isn't really *sexy,* is he?

NANCY. Oh, do shut up! (*To* DIANA, *gently, coaxingly.*) You're just so young to be getting in *wrong* with the world. Your allowance will be tiny and your social position absolutely *nil.* Your friends will all take sides and –

ACT ONE, SCENE TWO 17

She breaks off as DEBO (*twelve*) *enters, in riding clothes, delighted to see her elder sisters.*

DEBO. Honks and Naunce, you *Hons*! Have you come for Decca's birthday? She won't appreciate it, she's in a beastly funk. I had to beg her to come riding, and then the pony bucked her; I don't blame it!

She takes an apple from her pocket and flings herself down on the rug, talking between bites.

We saw the Hunger Marchers marching to London to see the Prime Minister, it was awfully sad. I howled!

NANCY. You *would.*

UNITY (*simultaneous*). Course you did.

DEBO. A long line of them – horribly tired and pale they looked, trudging along with enormous placards, even the children, singing a frightful dirge. Decca was all for joining them.

During the above JESSICA (*fifteen*) *has entered, hot and bothered, tugging at her riding gloves.*

JESSICA. I jolly well *would* have, if I hadn't been stuck with *you*! I wouldn't mind one bit, marching to Parliament with all those friendly people, singing songs.

UNITY. Boud, you can barely be bothered to walk to the post office.

JESSICA. It's different, Boud. (*Re: her gloves.*) Blast, these buttons!

DIANA. Come here, darling. It's because they're new, that's all.

JESSICA goes to DIANA, who unbuttons the gloves and slides them off easily. JESSICA *buries her hot face in* DIANA*'s collarbone.* NANCY *observes her critically.*

NANCY. What is she today, fifteen?

UNITY. Of course she's fifteen!

DIANA (*gently detatching* JESSICA). Happy birthday, darling.

DEBO. 'Happy' my eye! She simply won't buck up. I gave her my last liquorice twist and did my best impression of Ethel laying an egg –

She breaks off to perform a superb imitation of a hen in the final stages of laying an egg, a familiar but much appreciated party-piece. Everyone applauds apart from JESSICA.

All for nothing, see? She *aches* for our scoundrel cousin.

UNITY. What cousin? (*To* JESSICA.) You didn't tell me you were aching, Boud.

JESSICA. There's nothing to tell. (*To* DEBO.) And you can shut up!

DEBO (*delighted*). Edmond Romilly. I caught her in the airing cupboard kissing a page from *The Times* about him being expelled from Eton.

JESSICA. It's *Esmond*, and I wasn't kissing it, I was reading it.

DEBO. With your mouth? Do admit!

JESSICA. And it wasn't Eton, it was Wellington.

UNITY. Expelled! How topping! What did he do?

JESSICA (*to* DEBO). He wasn't expelled either, you'd make a hopeless spy. (*To* UNITY.) He ran away from Wellington, I expect because it was utterly bloody. *Then* he was expelled, for running away. Now he's set up a sort of camp for runaway boys in a Communist bookshop in London.

UNITY. Shame he's a Bolshie, he sounds rather a Hon!

JESSICA (*eagerly*). I think he *is,* Boud!

UNITY. If he's our cousin why don't we know him?

NANCY. Second cousin. I've met him.

JESSICA. When?

NANCY. At Chartwell. He's Winston Churchill's nephew, and a thoroughly charmless little rabble-rouser. I'd suggest you get over it, we've trouble enough as it is.

DEBO. What do you mean? What trouble?

NANCY. Look, you two are going to have to scram.

DEBO. But it's Decca's birthday!

NANCY. All day, I believe. Presents after tea.

JESSICA. This is our schoolroom, Heartless. We've things to do in here.

NANCY. Nothing you can't do elsewhere.

JESSICA (*to* DIANA). Honks, can I borrow your wedding ring?

DIANA. I'm afraid it's at Ospreys, darling, being resized.

JESSICA. That big sparkler then?

DIANA. Engagement ring? Whatever for?

DIANA slides the ring off, drops it into JESSICA's palm. JESSICA kisses her impulsively.

JESSICA. You're a Hon! It's just for carving, it won't hurt the diamond. We tried it with Muv's and it was fine.

NANCY. Can you carve whatever it is outside, please?

JESSICA. Can't, I'm afraid. Has to be here.

She goes to the window seat and kneels up on it, inspecting the glass.

UNITY (*to* NANCY). See, I've done acres of lovely swastikas on my side. Dec was to do hers this morning, but Muv came in and took her ring back.

DIANA. Does Muv know you two are carving swastikas into the windows?

JESSICA. *I'm* not carving swastikas. I'd sooner die.

DEBO. Dec's doing hammers-and-sickles.

NANCY. Well, you don't need to do them now. Push off, both of you.

JESSICA ignores her and starts carving into the glass with the ring.

DEBO. Why can Unity stay and not us?

UNITY. Because I know all about it already.

DEBO. About what?

NANCY. Never you mind.

JESSICA. But we do mind.

DIANA. Let them stay. They're bound to hear sooner or later.

DEBO. Hear what?

UNITY. Honks is going to bolt!

NANCY. Oh, for Heaven's sake!

DEBO. 'Bolt'?

UNITY. All right – Honks has fallen madly in love, and he's wild for her too, and she's going to leave Bryan and it's all perfectly *wondair*!

JESSICA stops carving, turns to stare at DIANA wide-eyed. DEBO fights back tears.

DEBO. It isn't true.

NANCY (*to* UNITY). Now you've done it.

UNITY. It's not my fault she's a cry-baby.

DEBO. Honks, *say it isn't true*!

She runs into DIANA's arms, sobbing. DIANA strokes her hair absently.

JESSICA (*to* DIANA, *troubled*). Will you get a divorce?

NANCY. Think very carefully. You'd be giving up everything.

DIANA. Gladly.

JESSICA. He must be jolly nice.

DIANA (*smiles*). He is.

UNITY. And jolly dishy!

NANCY. *He* won't give up a thing, you do realise that? Not his work, not his wife and children, nor his apparently countless mistresses!

DIANA. I don't want him to, least of all his work. He *is* his work.

JESSICA. He hasn't *mistresses,* has he?

NANCY. Of course he has – she *is* one!

DIANA. And I don't expect him to give up his family either. I shan't give up my children, why must he?

NANCY. Then what on earth do you propose to do?

DIANA. Buy a little house in London, and the babies and I shall live in it. And when Kit wants me, he'll come to me. I'm perfectly content to be on my own forever, so long as I can see him from time to time.

JESSICA. Kit's a queer sort of name.

DIANA. That's what I call him. Kitten.

NANCY. Oswald Mosley? A *kitten*?

    JESSICA *starts and drops the diamond ring. It clatters to the ground.*

JESSICA. Oswald Mosley? What's he to do with it?

UNITY. Keep up! That's who we're talking about, you risible Droudled Boudle! That's who Honks is going to bolt with!

JESSICA. *Mosley?* The Fascist?

UNITY. Wouldn't mind if she bolted with a Bolshie, would you?

JESSICA (*hotly*). I'd mind for poor old Bryan either way, but if she must bolt –

She turns to DIANA, *appalled.*

Oh Honks. Not *him.* Not *you.*

DIANA. But Kit's for the workers, darling – just like you! He's the one man in England who dares tell the truth about poverty – and challenge the system and look for a better way. Come to a meeting, you'll see.

UNITY. *I'll* come, golly, I'd die to! Might I, Honks?

JESSICA. And listen to hateful talk and get clobbered by Blackshirt thugs?

DIANA. There aren't any thugs, the newspapers make that up.

JESSICA. I've seen photographs! Beastly Fascists with wooden clubs –

DIANA. Darling, I've been to heaps of meetings and never seen anything but perfect civility. Might I have my ring back, if you've finished?

JESSICA *snatches the diamond up from the floor.*

JESSICA. I haven't, as it happens. I'm surprised you even want it now.

NANCY. It's worth a fortune. Give it back. (*To* DIANA.) You'll need every penny, if you go through with this.

DIANA. It's all right, she can play with it.

JESSICA. I'm not a child!

NANCY. Of course you are, you silly little ballroom Communist! Scratching pictures in the glass with diamonds isn't going to change the world.

JESSICA. I'm not a 'ballroom Communist', I'm a real one, or I shall be, just as soon as I can get away from *here*! And I *will* change the world, you see if I don't!

UNITY *cheers and stamps wildly.*

NANCY (*to* UNITY). I thought you were a Fascist.

ACT ONE, SCENE TWO 23

UNITY. To my very core – but she's my Boud, and it's her birthday, so we must be nice to her, even if she is The Enemy.

DIANA (*to* JESSICA). There's a thought. Why not open some presents?

JESSICA *shakes her head, distraught.* DIANA *looks around at all the tragic faces.*

Couldn't you be a little glad for me, darlings?

UNITY. *I'm* glad!

DIANA (*to the others*). Don't you see, I was so young when I met Bryan, and I thought that's what love *is* – a sweet, soft feeling, like one has for a brother. But then… I sat next to Kit at a supper party and –

She breaks off. DEBO *sits up. She has stopped crying and now looks decidedly interested.*

DEBO. And what?

DIANA. What, darling?

DEBO. You sat next to Kit and what happened?

DIANA. Oh. Well. Something else entirely.

DEBO. *What* entirely?

NANCY. Never you mind.

DEBO. I know what she's talking about. Even hedgehogs do it.

UNITY. Hedgehogs? (*She giggles, to* JESSICA.) Did you hear that, Boud?

DEBO. They do! The females flatten their spikes and the males snort and huff and puff like mad, I've seen it. Sometimes they roll about on their backs and give the ladies a tremendous display!

UNITY*'s giggles grow increasingly febrile and uncontrolled as* DEBO *warms to her theme.*

Making bodies. That's what it's about. You all pretend it's politics and welfare and hunger and taxation but really it's about making bodies. (*Pointing at* DIANA.) You want to Do It with Mr Mosley. (*At* UNITY.) You want to Do It with Mr Hitler. (*At* JESSICA.) You want to Do It with Lenin and Cousin Edmond.

JESSICA. Lenin's dead, you dunce. And it's *Esmond*.

DEBO (*to* NANCY). Even *you* want to Do It with all your pansy friends in London!

NANCY (*defiant*). As it happens, I'm dining with Peter Rodd on Saturday.

UNITY. Remember to flatten your spikes!

DEBO. Peter Rodd? The boring one?

DIANA (*swiftly, to* DEBO). What about you, dear? Aren't you aching for anyone?

DEBO. Not in the least, I think it's a frightful waste of time. I intend to run about and go riding and fishing and skating and have fun for as long as I can. Then, when I'm old enough, I shall marry a duke.

NANCY. A duke, indeed!

UNITY (*beside herself*). A duke!

DEBO. Yes, I'll marry a duke.

UNITY. Well, I hope he snorts and puffs and rolls about!

DIANA. Careful, darling, your dress – it's only pins –

There's a tearing sound as UNITY*'s dress comes apart at the seams, leaving her in grubby, ill-fitting underclothes. She steps free of it with a joyous wriggle and begins to sing. Like* DEBO*'s chicken impersonation, this is a familiar party-piece.*

UNITY (*sings*).
'I'm Sex Appeal Sarah,
my body grows barer,
each time I appear on a stage…'

Everyone but JESSICA *is laughing now.* UNITY *reaches out to her, appealing.*

Come on, Boud, now in Bouldedidge! (*She repeats the song in their private language.*) 'Eem dzegs abiddle Dzeeldra, my buddy grads beeldra, idge deedem ee adeeldron ge dzedge!'

She does a wild, comical dance, circling JESSICA *and reiterating the song until, unable to resist her,* JESSICA *joins in. They dance each other out of the room.* DEBO *can't bear it.*

DEBO. Wait for me!

She chases after them. Their singing is heard, off. NANCY *and* DIANA *listen, amused.*

NANCY. Infants!

DIANA. Well, they *are,* aren't they?

NANCY *takes a cigarette case from her pocket, offers it to* DIANA, *who takes one.*

NANCY. I wish *we* were, don't you?

DIANA. Infants?

NANCY. Awfully nice, not having to be all grown up and responsible.

DIANA. Being grown up can be rather nice too, you know.

NANCY (*scrutinising her*). Have you had *any sleep at all*?

DIANA *smiles;* NANCY *is drawn in despite herself.*

You'll get frightful crows' feet.

DIANA Worth it.

NANCY. That's not all you'll get.

DIANA. Still worth it; do admit.

NANCY. I'll take your word for it.

DIANA. You wait.

26   THE PARTY GIRLS

NANCY. I've *waited*, dear.

DIANA. Perhaps this Peter Rodd might be the chap.

NANCY. Perhaps. He's not precisely the hero of one's dreams, but still. How much can one reasonably expect?

DIANA. Everything. One ought to expect everything.

A beat.

NANCY. Honks, will you at least *think* about what I said?

DIANA (*soothingly*). Yes, darling…

Scene Three

1942. Bob's office, the Office of Price Administration, Washington. Night.

BOB *stands, cigarette in hand, over a complicated chart, moving tiny flags and pegs around.*

The radio plays. JESSICA (*twenty-five*) *walks past, laden with boxes. She stops and stares at him.*

JESSICA. Bob, what on earth are you doing? Everyone's gone home! You haven't even started packing, you might as well sleep under your desk – the removal men can throw you in the van tomorrow morning.

BOB. Take a look.

He divests her of the boxes and draws her to his desk. She considers the scale-plan keenly.

JESSICA. Are you going to invade Germany?

BOB. That's next.

JESSICA. Well, what is it?

BOB. It's the seating plan for the new office. I found it in a meeting room upstairs. Looks like we're all going to turn up at the new joint tomorrow to find our desks, typewriters, ashtrays – maybe even our cigarette butts – relocated in the *exact same position* as here.

JESSICA. Do you mind?

BOB. You don't think it's creepy?

JESSICA. So what are you up to?

BOB. A little mischief.

JESSICA. Tell me more.

BOB. Take this yellow flag, for instance. This represents, if you consult the key, that mean-spirited dame who's the Chair of the Ways and Means Committee. The lady is an unabashed racist, snob and antisemite.

JESSICA. I've encountered the lady.

BOB. So, I've plucked her out of her cosy corner of fellow-bigots and put her *here,* surrounded by Jews, Blacks and a couple of Judy Garland fans. Picture her face.

JESSICA. Bob, you're an anarchist!

BOB. Meanwhile, this gentleman here, blue flag, has been quietly drumming up support for the America First Committee. He likes to work in a dark corner where no one can see what he's up to; I've brought him right into the light.

JESSICA. Sterling work!

BOB. I also did a little matchmaking. I happen to know my secretary is crazy for one of the new attorneys – a bachelor, I checked – so I switched her desk to right outside his office. Ten cents, they're engaged by June.

JESSICA. What if she's not his type?

BOB. By June, she'll be his type.

JESSICA. And what about your wicked roommate?

BOB. That's the kicker. Ike will have to take three flights of stairs to even catch sight of a dame. Say – you won't rat on me, will you?

JESSICA. What price silence?

BOB. Name it, sister.

JESSICA. Might I have a crack at some mischief?

BOB. Be my guest!

> JESSICA *pores eagerly over the seating plan. She plucks up a flag, refers to the key.*

JESSICA. All right. That Richard chap in Legal. Looks like Boris Karloff, always eats lunch on his own.

BOB. Richard Nixon. (*Amused.*) 'Boris Karloff'…

JESSICA. Strikes me as something of a right-winger. And he seems a little too comfy in his current situation. I'd like to move Boris Karloff – (*She demonstrates.*) here. Into what I believe to be a nest of parlour pinks or, as an acquaintance of mine used to say, 'Ballroom Communists', where he might find his ideas a tad more challenged. Well? What do you say?

BOB. I say let's drink to that.

He seizes a bottle of whisky, pours a couple of shots.

JESSICA. Just a drop for me. Dinky's entertaining tonight.

BOB. Dinky's always entertaining.

JESSICA. This time it's a starchy British nanny who'll be unimpressed by me, bowling home at ten o'clock, reeking of spirits. (*Raises her glass.*) To mischief!

BOB. Mischief!

> JESSICA *takes a slug of her drink, regarding him keenly.*

JESSICA. So are they? 'Parlour pinks'? That little gang?

BOB. They sure blush easy.

JESSICA (*amused*). You're not going to tell me, are you.

BOB (*all innocence*). Tell you what?

JESSICA. All right then – explain to me. Why is the Party so underground here? Aside from a few right-wingers, most of our colleagues seem to think and feel the same way about the world. You and I do – don't we? Yet one can't seem to say the word Comm–

He puts a finger to his lips, half-playful. She fractionally lowers her voice.

Or think of a single soul one might ask about joining.

BOB. Are you asking me?

She looks at him steadily.

I support Party causes from the outside. I'm not a member.

JESSICA. But – in principle?

BOB. In principle… I should've signed up years ago.

JESSICA (*exultant*). I knew it!

BOB. My first job, I was apprenticed to the Ladies Garment Workers' Union; representing the Embroiderers, Pleaters, Tuckers and Tubular Piping Workers of New York. Among other things, I helped them write a musical –

JESSICA. A *musical*?

BOB. For a fundraiser; we called it *Pins and Needles* – it was a smash. Then the Union president said we had to give a benefit performance for 'brave little Finland' –

JESSICA. Fascist little Finland, more like!

BOB. That's how the actors felt, and when I suggested we vote on it, the Union president said, 'Bob, you're a goddamn Communist!' I ran to the library, took out every book I could find on the subject, and what do you know – I am. But somehow… I never got around to joining.

JESSICA. Esmond and I, the same. We were on the point of it when he was called up. He said he'd join in England, and that I should get on and join here. But I didn't know who to ask. So…

A beat.

BOB. I might have a contact.

JESSICA. You might?

BOB. What do you say?

They catch eyes, excited; hold the gaze a beat too long.

JESSICA. The only fly being – in this particular ointment – that perhaps I ought to wait for Esmond. So we can do it together. In case he didn't, over there.

BOB. Sure. What's the rush?

JESSICA. You don't think I'm kidding myself, like everyone else does? Even his mother's stopped thinking he's alive. Even the Dink has taken to giving me pitying looks –

BOB. Now you're being paranoid. Dinky looks at everyone like that.

JESSICA. You see, I've always *known,* with Esmond. Everything. I knew I'd fall in love with him before I even met him, and I knew he'd love me back. Of course, I was jolly nervous he might not, but underneath, I had this absolute – I *knew.* So surely I'd know if he…if… Wouldn't I?

BOB. I don't know. But like most of my tribe, I'm kind of a melancholy optimist. Against my better judgement, I believe in hope.

He lifts his glass. She responds in kind.

JESSICA. It's a queer thing, you know; in England, people don't talk about being Jewish. One knows who is, or assumes one does, but they never mention it, or make a feature of it. You do. I like that.

BOB. Over here, as you noticed, we don't shout from the roof about being Reds. I like it that you do, too.

JESSICA. Sing me one of the songs. You know – 'Pins and Needles'.

BOB. Not on your life!

JESSICA. Be a sport!

He shakes his head, laughing, takes a hefty swig of his drink.

BOB. I'll tell you a poem I wrote, if you like.

JESSICA. What about?

BOB. You, as it happens.

JESSICA. Me?

He clears his throat, raises his glass. JESSICA *waits, intrigued.*

BOB. Drink a drink to Dauntless Decca
OPA's black-market wrecker
Where there is no violation
She provides the provocation
Smiling brightly, she observes,
'Je suis agente provocateuse!'

JESSICA *applauds, delighted. He grins modestly.*

JESSICA. Dauntless Decca! Bob, I adore it! No one's ever written a poem about me, not since I was a little girl, putting on Christmas concerts with my sist– with –

She breaks off. BOB *frowns carefully down at his seating plan.*

I must dash, that nanny will be simply seething. Do go home at some point, won't you?

BOB. But I'm having such fun.

She pauses, leaning over the plan.

JESSICA. Where am I, by the way? I can't see myself.

BOB. You're here, Dauntless. Right by me. Unless – I mean, of course, you can sit anywhere you like –

JESSICA (*warmly*). We're going to be tremendous pals, aren't we, Bob?

Scene Four

September 1969. Nancy's bedroom, Versailles, France. Afternoon.

DEBO *(forty-nine) is sorting through a tray of pills.* DIANA *(fifty-nine) sits on the bed, holding the telephone, waiting as it rings. The television quietly plays an Elvis Presley film,* Blue Hawaii. DEBO *holds up a bottle of pills.*

DEBO. What about these? Sleep or pain?

DIANA. Let's see? (*She squints at them.*) Pain.

DEBO. I thought pink were pain.

DIANA. Mild pain; those are strongling.

DEBO. How many max?

DIANA. Dr Gauchet said up to six per day –

DEBO. *Six?*

DIANA. One thing I've learned, living in France, is that the docs love to knock out their patients. I rather enjoy it. Naunce loathes it, she says it makes her hallucinate and then she can't write her book.

DEBO. I'd have thought it would help; lovely flights of fancy –

DIANA. It's a memoir of Frederick the Great, dear.

DEBO *writes on a pad of paper.*

DEBO. '*Strongling* painkillers, six max.' I keep forgetting it's Fred the Great. Who on earth will want to read that?

DIANA. You'd be surprised.

DEBO. I *would.* (*Re: phone.*) Is it ringing?

DIANA. He must be in the garden. He grows all our veg now – (*Into phone.*) Kit! Were you in the garden, darling? (*Louder.*) Were you in the garden?… I hope you haven't trodden mud into my Aubusson. (*Louder.*) My *carpet,* darling… Yes, still at Nancy's. She's *wondair* today. Slept until ten, no pain to speak of, and she's got the Colonel here. They've been shut away in the drawing room for hours… (*Laughing.*) Kit! I very much doubt it. At any rate, I shall run Debo in to Paris and whizz home, I should be in Orsay before supper… She's very well. She's making me watch an awful Elvis Presley film because she's got the hots for him.

DEBO. Not just the hots, he's a musical genius.

DIANA (*into phone*). A musical genius, apparently. (*To* DEBO.) Kit says you're mad and sends love.

DEBO (*calling*). Oodles of love back!

DIANA (*to phone*). She sends hers. I'll see you tonight, darling… Neither can I. It feels like simply aeons. (*Louder.*) Like aeons. Bye, my love.

She replaces the receiver. For a moment, they watch the Elvis film.

DEBO. He is dishy. Do admit.

DIANA. I can't see it.

DEBO. I never could either! But then I caught an interview after Bobby Kennedy was shot, and Elvis was so darling about him, I was in floods. Then he picked up his guitar and sang, 'If I Can Dream', you know, in tribute – and wham! (*She clutches her heart.*) A thunderbolt! You know how one suddenly *gets it*?

DIANA. What does Andrew make of your little pash?

DEBO. Andrew, being a perfect Hon, has got concert tickets for my dreaded fiftieth and acquired a backstage pass! The children say they're going to leak it to the *News of the World* – 'Duchess of Devonshire to meet The King'.

DIANA. Not for the first time. Different King, of course.

DEBO. Rather sexier, no offence to his Late Highness.

DIANA. You are lucky. Kit gets simply green if I fancy someone else. He flatly refuses to watch a David Niven film, or even let me go on my own.

DEBO. I think that's sweet. Was he all right?

DIANA. Keen to have me home. He hadn't his ears in, which makes it rather a strain. One has to say everything twice in exactly the same tone of voice so he doesn't feel ticked off, poor lamb.

DEBO. You are a saint, Honks. Sure it's not a bind, taking me to the airport?

DIANA. Worth it for the extra sister-time.

DEBO. I do feel beastly, going back to England.

DIANA. Well, you mustn't. It's been bliss to have you out here but it's time to get back to your own life. There's going to be plenty of this.

DEBO. I know.

DIANA. With any luck Pam will come out again at Christmas and in the meantime – Decca seems to genuinely want to do her bit.

DEBO. I'm just not sure nursing is Decca's strong point, are you?

DIANA. I couldn't begin to say.

DEBO. I don't suppose she's had much experience of emptying bedpans and mopping fevered brows. Even when the children were small… I always had the impression *he* did most of the mothering.

DIANA. She only has to keep Naunce cheerful and administer the drugs. She needn't be Florence Nightingale.

DEBO. Every time I ring up to brief her, she's rushing out to be interviewed by *Life Magazine* or appear on *The Ed Sullivan Show*. Or address a gala dinner on the importance of Black Power, or the anguish of growing up in the Cotswolds –

DIANA *is laughing.*

It's true! Then, when one finally does get through, it's impossible to make her listen to the dull practicalities. Her voice goes all faraway and one can hear the typewriter very faintly clacking.

DIANA. Poor Dec, she just wants to make sure you don't forget she's terribly grown up and important now. I'm sure she's taking in every word.

DEBO. Well, I've written it all down in case. Have a squiz.

She passes DIANA *her notepad, peering over her shoulder as she scans it.*

That's all the medication. Instructions for meals and housekeeping, money for Cook and the girl. And the full regiment of docs and their telephone numbers.

DIANA (*drily*). And mine, I notice.

DEBO. I've told her she must absolutely ring you up if anything goes wrong.

DIANA. She'll make sure it doesn't, then.

DEBO (*wistful*). I can't help secretly hoping it might be like a French farce, you know; the two of you dashing in and out of different doors and Naunce inventing wild ruses to keep you apart. Then in the final act you bump into each other and everyone's in floods and all's forgiven.

DIANA. Well, I intend to spend the week at home, reading and gardening and giving some attention to Kit. I shan't expect to hear from Decca unless there's an emergency, which please God there won't be.

The front door slams, off. They look at each other conspiratorially.

DEBO. He's gone. I hope he gave her a good time.

DIANA. That's what Kit said! I'm not sure she's ready for a good time just yet.

DEBO. She was awfully excited when he pitched up. Clouds of *Mitsouko*! She still seems to find him irresistible; I can't think why.

DIANA. I wish she didn't. I'm fond of the Colonel, but he does have a tendency to scram when he feels leaned upon.

DEBO. Do you suppose if he knew how unwell –

DIANA. I think it's certainly best we keep it *entre nous.*

DEBO. Which is my other worry about Decca. You know how she prides herself on being a whistle-blower, or whatever it is they call her.

DIANA. 'Queen of the Muckrakers'.

DEBO. She doesn't think we should be keeping anything *entre nous.*

DIANA. I see her point. It's frightful, knowing more than Nancy.

DEBO. But the specialist said –

DIANA. Keep her spirits up, I know. Frightful, all the same.

DEBO. Yes, one just hopes Decca doesn't suddenly decide to, you know –

She blows an invisible whistle. NANCY (*sixty-five*) *enters. She's all tailored elegance but frail. Walking costs her, though she's at pains to disguise it. She holds a bottle of champagne.*

NANCY (*breezy, to* DEBO). Are you calling the hounds?

DEBO. Wouldn't that be nice!

NANCY. The Colonel sends his regards. I told him to come up but he scuttled off like a frightened penguin. (*Holding out the champagne.*) Have some of this, it's heavenly. I can't drink another drop.

DIANA *takes the champagne from her.* NANCY *perches on the bed, lights a cigarette.*

DEBO. What were you celebrating?

NANCY. My clean bill of health, of course. And the Colonel's news.

DIANA. His news?

ACT ONE, SCENE FOUR 37

NANCY. Yes, he brought news.

They look at her, expectant.

DEBO. Well, what was it?

NANCY. Wedding bells! A blushing groom at barely seventy!

DIANA. He's getting *married*? To whom?

NANCY. You've gone quite white. Not getting one of your migraines, are you?

DIANA. Not that dreary Countess?

DEBO. Countess?

NANCY. 'Violette de Talleyrand-Périgord'. Keep up, Debo. He's been flitting between the two of us for years.

DEBO. I've never even heard of her.

NANCY. She's not very interesting, that's why. A divorcée, like me, only in her case he suddenly doesn't seem to mind. God will apparently forgive.

DIANA (*stricken*). Oh Naunce! How could he?

DEBO. You mustn't be on speakers with him ever again!

NANCY. Darlings, it's not that bad. He never promised anything.

DIANA. But why must he come here and tell you all about it? It's cruel of him, unbearably cruel!

NANCY. Because we're the best of friends and he wanted to tell me himself. The announcement will be in *Le Figaro* tomorrow morning, he didn't want me to choke on my egg. Rather Honnish, I thought.

DIANA. I shall never forgive him. To do this to you, at a time like this –

NANCY. Like what? I'm full of the joys! And grateful to be alive and mostly out of pain. *Do* forgive – I did at once. He's coming for tea tomorrow.

DEBO. Naunce, you oughtn't to let him!

NANCY. Why? I'd be devastated if he stopped coming to see me simply because he's going to marry someone else. The only crucial thing is that I need to get back to my book, and that's why we must put off Decca.

She busies herself amongst her books and papers.

DEBO. Put off Decca?

NANCY. Yes, I'm horribly behind. Someone sent me a cutting from *The Bookseller,* 'Nancy Mitford's *imminent* biography' –

DEBO. But, Naunce – she's on her way!

NANCY. Well, she must be stopped. Turned back.

DIANA. From *California,* darling, be reasonable. She's in mid-air! Besides, with Debo leaving, and I simply *must* have a few days at home –

NANCY. Of course you must! I never dreamed you should stay all this time! You've been marvellous, both of you, but I'm in fine fettle now. I'm sorry if Decca has made plans, but –

DEBO. She'll be here tomorrow, first thing!

NANCY. Then she can have a lovely French holiday, but she shall have to put up elsewhere. I can't have her. I've far too much to do and –

A sudden wave of pain in her back and legs makes her reel. DIANA *and* DEBO *leap to support her, helping her to a chair. She closes her eyes.*

It's a twinge, that's all. It's passing.

DIANA (*gently*). But this is why you must have someone here, dear.

NANCY. I do have someone.

DEBO. We don't mean Cook or the girl –

NANCY. I have Fred.

DEBO. Fred?

DIANA. She means Frederick the Great.

The pain has receded. NANCY *opens her eyes, smiles calmly at her sisters.*

NANCY. Nothing matters as long as I'm writing. If I'm writing, I can bear it. Anything. But I must have *peace.* I can't have Decca hovering at my back when I'm trying to work. I can't have endless conversations about how her life was blighted because we weren't allowed to go to school and the rest of you turned into Nazis.

DEBO. *I* didn't turn into a –

DIANA (*laughs*). Naunce, you're wicked.

NANCY. Do admit. She's made a jolly good career of being the revolutionary, but she can't have it both ways. She's either part of this family or at war with it. There's no earthly point her coming if she isn't *one of us.*

Scene Five

Washington, 1942. A little alcove in the Troika nightclub/bar.

JESSICA (*twenty-five*) *sits at a table, shaken, flexing a slightly bruised hand. In the other she holds a professional-looking camera.* BOB *approaches with drinks. She raises the camera.*

JESSICA. Say 'cheese'.

BOB. 'Philadelphia.'

She snaps the camera at him.

I thought you ripped the film out.

JESSICA. I did.

BOB. It suits you. Perhaps he'll let you keep it.

JESSICA. I don't suppose he's awfully keen to come and get it.

BOB. I'll ask one of the girls to send it to his office. Maybe fix it up so it explodes.

He puts down the drinks and studies her.

You okay, Dauntless?

JESSICA. I'm fine. Hand's a bit sore, that's all.

BOB. Can you wiggle your fingers?

BOB *scoops ice from his glass, wraps it in his handkerchief, presses it to her knuckles. She inhales sharply.*

Does it hurt?

She shakes her head. He continues to hold the ice there.

I heard the boss took it well.

JESSICA. I thought he was going to sack me on the spot, but he just patted me on the shoulder and told me to go home and rest. He didn't even ask me to explain. Everyone's been terribly kind. Which makes it even –

She breaks off, draws her hand away, fighting tears of shame.

BOB. Dec, you did nothing wrong.

JESSICA. I punched a man in the face and stole his camera!

BOB. Good for you! The guy was a creep! A sleazy hack who sneaked into a federal building under false pretences and –

JESSICA. Could we talk about something else, Bob?

A beat.

Distract me. Tell me something funny.

BOB. Okay… Guess who told me last night that he doesn't want to play the field any more? Wants to settle down?

JESSICA (*half-listening*). Go on.

BOB. Three guesses.

ACT ONE, SCENE FIVE 41

JESSICA. I don't know.

BOB. Ike! He's had an epiphany! He's in love with Joyce – the girl who left – and he wants her back, only Joyce won't take his calls. So, last night, couple of bourbons; we come up with a plan. You know those do-it-yourself gramophones you can buy? Write your own songs and record them? We came up with a cute little number. (*Sings.*) 'Dear Joyce, please come to Washington, Ike wants to marry you. Dear – '

JESSICA (*suddenly*). I knew that man had come for me the moment I saw him. I was heading for the lobby – looking for *you,* in point of fact – and there he was, asking questions. Snooping around. I turned and started to walk away but he'd seen me. He came after me, pushed in front of me, snapping that wretched camera in my face. (*American accent.*) 'Say, Decca, you ever call home? How's your sisters? Say, are your parents Nazis too? Is it true your sister Unity was conceived in a Canadian town called Swastika?' (*Dropping the accent.*) It *is,* by the way.

BOB. Wait, what?

JESSICA. On and on, question after question. My family, my childhood, he seemed to know it all. And how could I explain, 'Yes, my father *did* set his hounds on us, but it was a game, the dogs would sooner die than hurt us, and Nancy wrote about it because it was funny, it was *funny,* and we loved it!' When he said that about Farve… I simply saw red.

BOB. Decca, you were right to sock the guy.

JESSICA. But I ought to have told *you*!

BOB (*lightly*). Told me? No one's talking about anything else. 'Decca decked a reporter' – it's all over the building.

JESSICA. You know what I mean.

He goes to speak but she holds up a hand to stop him.

No, listen. You've been the most wonderful friend to the Dink and me, these past few months. And I've wanted to be honest with you, truly I have, but every time I – choked on it. Whenever you spoke about your family – all I could think was, my God. *My sisters.*

BOB. Are your sisters. They're not you, any more than my sister is me.

JESSICA. I can't imagine Edith is a member of the Third Reich.

BOB. And if she was? Would it make me one? Or make me in any way responsible for what she chooses to believe?

JESSICA. What about your mother?

BOB. I don't think she's one.

JESSICA. What would she *say*? About us being chums?

BOB. My mother would love you. She's dying to meet you.

JESSICA. She might be less keen when she finds out –

BOB. She *knows,* Dec.

JESSICA. What?

BOB. Everyone knows.

She stares at him, confused.

How could we not? You and Esmond hit the society pages from the day you landed – he had a column in the *Washington Post*!

JESSICA. For five minutes! As Romilly, *never* Mitford!

BOB. We knew. And it didn't make a jot of difference to any one of us – least of all me.

JESSICA. But – why didn't you *say something*?

BOB. Like what? You told me you had no sisters, I figured you didn't want to talk about them and no kidding – I could see why! So I let it be.

JESSICA. Let me carry on pretending, making an utter fool of myself –

BOB. You never, for one moment, made a fool –

JESSICA. I didn't need to, did I? You were doing it for me!

BOB. Hey, that's not fair –

She jumps to her feet.

JESSICA. I'll tell you what's not fair! You – knowing more about my life than I ever chose to tell you! Reading about my family in the ghastly press and laughing behind my back – it's worse than unfair, it's bloody cruel!

BOB. Where are you going?

JESSICA. Anywhere that isn't here!

She grabs for her coat, storms towards the exit; then stops. A beat. She returns to the table and sits, not looking at BOB. *He pours a glass of water, pushes it across to her.*

I hate water.

BOB. Drink it anyway. And breathe.

JESSICA. I hate breathing.

BOB. Sure, but we got to do it. Otherwise Hitler has us licked.

She takes a reluctant sip of water. A jazz band strikes up close by and people start dancing, out of view. They sit quietly for a moment, then:

JESSICA. When I was twelve, I set up a running-away account at Drummonds' Bank. It was actually called that, on all the official statements and everything, 'The Honourable Jessica Mitford's Running-Away Account'. I always knew, you see, one day I'd have to scram.

BOB. From what?

JESSICA. All of it. Their politics and their snobbery, their privilege – and I *loved* privilege, Bob. Loved clothes and jewellery and scent as much as any other silly debutante – and loathed it too, and loathed myself for loving it. I used all my savings to scram to Spain with Esmond.

BOB. To fight Franco?

JESSICA. You bet. First night, we were in a café, and a rough-looking chap came in with a big old dog on a chain and started whipping it, right across its face. People were laughing and egging him on – I was beside myself. I was screaming, 'Esmond, for God's sake, *do* something', and he grabbed my wrist and dragged me outside. Talk about furious!

BOB. Sure, to beat an animal –

JESSICA. No, with *me*!

BOB. You?

JESSICA. 'How *dare* you impose your beastly English upper-class preoccupations on a place you can't begin to understand? That's why you're so detested abroad, because you have the nerve to come to other countries and tell them how to treat their dogs!' I hadn't seen him lose his rag before; we were virtually strangers. He was shaking. 'Don't you realise that's how the English upper-classes treat *human beings* – in India and Africa and all over the world? If you're going to make such a fuss, you ought to have stayed at home, where they grill sirloins for their dogs, and let the people in the slums starve to death!'

BOB. But – isn't Esmond upper-class himself?

JESSICA. He is! I mean – he was. He was.

A beat, as this lands for them both. She straightens up.

Would you care to dance, Bob? You can say no, I shan't mind. In England it's not at all the done thing, for the girl to ask the fellow.

BOB. I'd care to. Very much.

JESSICA. Not out there, though. It's awfully bright.

BOB. Let's dance right here.

They stand, step cautiously into each other's arms. They hold each other lightly, aware of their proximity, but as they start to dance, they are simply, naturally in step. The music changes, becomes more intimate. She steps back, suddenly formal.

You okay, Dec? Want to sit down?

JESSICA. Thank you, no. That was perfectly lovely. I must get home.

Scene Six

The schoolroom, Swinbrook, 1935.

DEBO (*fifteen*) *is having her nails painted by* DIANA (*twenty-five*). UNITY (*twenty-one*), *in a fever of excitement, puts up postcards of Hitler all around the room.*

UNITY. Honks, tell her, wasn't it too funny about the lipstick?

DIANA. You tell, darling, this takes heaps of concentration.

DEBO (*to* UNITY). Go on, tell.

UNITY. You see, last year my friend Putzi said that Honks and I couldn't under any circs come to the *Parteitag* –

DEBO. The what?

DIANA. The rally, you know, in Nuremberg.

UNITY. Because we wear too much lipstick! Or at least, we couldn't be introduced to the Führer because he can't tolerate too much make-up on a woman.

DEBO. Why not?

UNITY. Putzi says he likes the more natural look, and I took him at his word because he and Hitler are bosom chums, and I hadn't met Hitler yet. But *this* year, of course –

DEBO. Hitler sounds just like Farve! Remember when Naunce got her hair bobbed? I thought Farve was going to burst!

UNITY. Do stop interrupting, Hitler's absolutely nothing like Farve.

DEBO (*to* DIANA). And when you left poor Bryan! 'Out! Out! I forbid you the house!' He'd be hopping mad if he knew you were here now.

DIANA. Well, he's in London, and he doesn't, so we're all safe.

UNITY. The point *is,* this year everything was different because we were there as Hitler's guests, and we told him the whole lipstick story and he thought it was killing! Didn't he roar, Honks?

DIANA. He *was* tickled that he'd been protected from our Max Factor Reds when he actually has to spend a lot of time with terribly mannish women who don't make any effort at all.

DEBO. You mean he does like lipstick after all? Why did Putzi lie?

UNITY. It wasn't a *lie.* It's simply that people believe Hitler to be so much more serious than he really is. Just because he doesn't drink or smoke or eat meat, and wants everyone to get lashings of fresh air and exercise, they always paint him as a prude. But he isn't at all – he's awfully jolly and doesn't mind a bit what other people do.

DEBO. Why is he always with mannish women?

DIANA. Oh, because of his work, you know. Government types and old maid secretaries with the kind of sturdy calves that Farve thought *we'd* get if we went to school and had to play hockey.

JESSICA (*eighteen*) *has entered in time to hear this.*

JESSICA. And I for one will never forgive Farve for it! I've got sturdy calves anyway, and I'd care a lot less if I had an education to go with them.

DEBO. Look, Dec, I'm having a moon manicure. It's like a French manicure, but the half-moons are the other way up.

JESSICA *ignores her, taking in what* UNITY *is doing.*

ACT ONE, SCENE SIX   47

JESSICA. How many of these repulsive postcards do you have?

UNITY. Three hundred and six, if you must know.

JESSICA. You don't even live here any more. Why don't you put them up in Munich, then Debo and I shan't have to look at them all the time?

UNITY. Come and visit, you'll see why.

DIANA. It's wall-to-wall Führer already, darling.

DEBO. He looks a bit miffed in most of them. I thought you said he was fun?

DIANA. He's quite different in real life. He has the loveliest eyes.

JESSICA. Perhaps I *shall* come and visit.

UNITY. I should love that! And he so wants to meet you!

DEBO. Don't wear lipstick though, he doesn't like it.

JESSICA. I shall wear so much that he drops down dead.

UNITY turns from her postcards to slowly look at JESSICA.

UNITY. You missed the lipstick story. It was actually funny.

JESSICA. Sounds *hilaire.*

UNITY. Oh Boud, can't you enjoy things a little? I was so looking forward to coming home and sharing everything with you. I didn't realise you'd tragically lost your sense of humour whilst we were away.

She bounds on to a chair, clutching a scarf as a surplice and speaking in a booming voice.

Dearly beloved, we are gathered here today to mark the untimely passing of the Honourable Jessica Mitford's Sense of Humour!

DEBO (*tears springing*). Don't!

DIANA. She's teasing, darling.

UNITY. Yea, though we walk through the valley of the shadow of death, we shall ne'er forget the sweet sunshiny days when Decca's laughter rippled out across the village green –

DEBO. Stop it!

UNITY. Poor Sense of Humour. So young to die.

JESSICA. Luckily it gets to share the family crypt with your Sense of Decency.

DEBO. Don't *you* start!

JESSICA. Room in there for yours too, Honks.

DIANA (*unperturbed*). Mine too?

JESSICA. Decency. You were at Nuremberg too.

UNITY. And we had a heavenly time without you!

DIANA. Girls, don't be spiteful. Unity goes back to Munich on Sunday and we all know how much you've missed each other. Try not to waste the time you have. There's nothing to cry about, Debo. Look at your pretty nails.

DEBO (*charmed*). Oh! Do you suppose they'll be spoiled when I feed the pigs?

DIANA. I'm afraid so, unless you wear gloves.

DEBO. But then the darling pigs shan't see them.

DEBO *dances about, admiring her hands.*

DIANA (*to* JESSICA). Want me to do yours?

JESSICA *stares at* DIANA, *confused by her.*

Three seconds to decide. One, two –

JESSICA. All right.

DIANA. Come here then.

JESSICA *obeys.* DIANA *prepares her workstation to start again.*

Pink and white or red and coral?

ACT ONE, SCENE SIX   49

UNITY. For a Bolshie? Need you ask?

JESSICA (*ignoring her*). Pink and white, please.

DEBO. That's what I've got. Pink and white's heaps nicer.

DIANA *rubs cream into* JESSICA*'s hands;* DEBO *watches admiringly. A tranquil lull.*

Do you think Farve will ever forgive you, Honks?

DIANA. Oh *yes*…

DEBO. I do hope so. I like it when you're here.

DIANA. Muv's already come halfway round. You ought to have seen her face when we took her to lunch at Claridges. Trying her best to stay cross when Kit was being so utterly sweet and beguiling.

JESSICA. Did she have to call him 'the Leader'?

DEBO. Of course not, silly. Muv's not a Blackshirt.

UNITY. Yet!

She steps back and admires her Hitler handiwork.

There. Isn't that nice?

JESSICA. Divine. Only one can't help wondering, amongst all the jolly japes, whether your friend the Führer ever mentions his plans for the Jews?

UNITY. Oh, the Jews, the Jews! Why must it always be about the Jews?

JESSICA. I expect they're wondering the same.

DIANA. Keep your hands still, darling, if you can.

UNITY. He wants rid of them, like we all do. Only in this country, no one dares do anything about it. We simply put up with it, like the weather. But Hitler's not afraid to tell the truth – in fact, he can't lie, can he, Honks?

DIANA (*gently, patiently, to* JESSICA). The point is, there are plenty of other places where they could go. Such a tremendous lot came in from Eastern Europe, after the war, and the poor Germans have borne the cost of them ever since.

JESSICA. Why do they cost anything? They're hard workers, aren't they?

DIANA. And they're mostly terribly successful. They can apply themselves to practically anything, and they're jolly clever at absorbing themselves into society. So why don't they go to America, or one of the countries that would *like* to have them? And leave Germany to the Germans.

JESSICA. They *are* Germans! They're German Jews!

DEBO. Farve says Jews would take the pennies from a dead man's eyes.

JESSICA. Well, Farve's a racialist and a bigot too!

DIANA *stops and lays her palms on* JESSICA*'s hands.*

DIANA. It's not easy to do this if you tremble so much.

DEBO (*to* JESSICA). Think about nice things. Piglets! Hot buttered toast.

JESSICA. I can't help it, Honks, it makes me feel so strange. Like my insides are melting and everything's draining away.

DIANA. You mustn't worry about the Jews. They're very resourceful people. It's merely a question of redistribution. No one's suggesting shooting them!

UNITY. I wouldn't mind! I've bought myself this natty little pistol and I'm learning. Make a bit of *lebensraum,* as the Führer says.

DEBO. A bit of what?

UNITY. Living space!

She cocks and fires an imaginary pistol.

See a few off, bang-bang.

JESSICA (*to* DIANA). Did you hear what she said?

DIANA. She's *teasing* you – when will you learn?

UNITY. I'm not, you know.

JESSICA (*to* UNITY). Besides, you're nothing but a copy-cat! You don't do anything unless Honks does it first. She bolts with Mosley and you become a Blackshirt – she learns German and you –

UNITY. What absolute bilge! It was *me* who went to live in Munich, and found out where Hitler takes his lunch and sat there every day until he had to notice me! It was *me* who introduced Honks! Tell her, Honks!

DIANA. Stop it, both of you. (*To* JESSICA.) She's old enough to make up her own mind about politics.

DEBO (*loyal*). So is Decca!

DIANA. Decca hasn't been to Germany, darling. One has to go there, talk to people, to understand how much Hitler's achieved already –

JESSICA. Talk to whom? Not the Jews, that's for sure!

UNITY. Everyone worships him! Little old ladies kneeling in the street to kiss his hand – we saw it, didn't we, Honks?

DIANA (*to* JESSICA). You know, Kit says England is on the brink of ruin, and he's right – for millions of families – no jobs, no welfare, beggars on the streets in London, freezing to death outside Harrods!

JESSICA. What does that have to do with –

DIANA. Because Germany was the same – worse! And now look! Employment's up, roads and hospitals are being built – and the public mood is simply marvellous! I can't tell you what it was like at the rally – the feeling of hope and possibility – perfect strangers embracing like friends because their country's coming back to life before their eyes! And Kit believes if it could happen there, it could happen *here.*

JESSICA. Of course he does! 'Britain First!', says the Leader! Make it impossible for the Jews to live and work and suddenly everything's *wondair*!

UNITY. Sacrifices must be made! If your Bolshie chums had their way, first for the chop would be *us*! Out with the aristocracy, off with our heads! It would be Muv and Farve and people like us on the guillotine!

DEBO (*horrified*). The guillot–

DIANA (*swiftly*). Not the guillotine.

UNITY. Why should we pay for *their* crimes?

JESSICA. *What* crimes?

UNITY. Boud, how can you be so blind? Listen –

She pulls a newspaper clipping from her pocket and reads aloud with passion.

'Dear sirs, as a British woman Fascist, I should like to express my admiration for you. I have lived in Munich for a year now and I read *Der Stürmer* every week.'

DEBO. What's *Der Stürmer*?

UNITY. 'If only we had such a newspaper in England. The English have no notion of the Jewish danger. Our worst Jews work only behind the scenes –

JESSICA. Behind the scenes at *what*? What on earth do you think they're *doing*?

She makes a futile grab for the cutting. UNITY *raises it high above her head.*

UNITY. Everything, idiot! Pulling the strings! Pretending to be humble and grateful to this country, crawling about amongst us like lice and secretly, secretly rising to power wherever one looks! Controlling everything – the newspapers, the stocks and shares, the government!

JESSICA. *How?* What are they, magicians? Lots of them are dirt-poor –

UNITY. And the rest are stinking rich, isn't that so, Honks? Oh, they can change their names and read *Debretts* and some of them can *pass* –

JESSICA (*to* DIANA). You don't believe this rot, do you?

DIANA. I wouldn't put it quite like that, but –

UNITY (*reads*). 'But we will soon win against this world enemy, despite all his cunning. We think with joy of the day we shall be able to say with might and authority: England for the English! Out with the Jews!'

JESSICA makes another grab for the cutting. UNITY *whisks it upwards in a Nazi salute.*

Seig Heil!

JESSICA. Oh Boud! What's happened to you?

UNITY. I'm having a bit of fun, that's all, remember fun?

JESSICA. Pin the tail on the Jew? What larks!

UNITY. I think you're jealous! I think you're perfectly green! Just because Honks and I have had a *wondair* experience, and met heaps of people, and we're getting away from this dismal place –

DEBO (*tears starting*). Swinbrook isn't dismal! What do you mean?

UNITY. And being part of something *extrorder* – a great wave of change that's going to transform the whole world – and making ourselves useful to a great man! (*She reads.*) 'Please publish my name in full, I want everyone to know that I am a Jew-hater' – and they did, look – (*She waves it at* JESSICA.) – wasn't that heavenly of them? I shall have it framed!

JESSICA makes a final lunge for the cutting and this time succeeds. DEBO *squeaks in alarm.* JESSICA *tears it into bits and throws them at* UNITY, *who stares at her, incensed.*

UNITY. My only copy. Honks, did you see?

DIANA. Stop this at once, both of you.

JESSICA. She began it!

DIANA. Well, that's not very grown up, is it?

UNITY picks up JESSICA's bust of Lenin. She holds her gaze, daring her.

JESSICA. You wouldn't.

UNITY hurls the bust to the ground. It smashes. She dances excitedly on the spot. And now all hell breaks loose as she and JESSICA wreak havoc on each other's possessions, hurling books, records, pamphlets, flags, as DEBO cowers in the corner and DIANA ineffectually attempts to intercede. Sudden blackness. Bombs crash and blaze, and air-raid sirens scream.

End of Act One.

ACT TWO

Scene One

New Year's Eve, 1942. The lobby of Bob's Washington apartment.

A party is taking place, off. JESSICA (*twenty-five*) *is buttoning her coat to leave.* BOB *enters.*

BOB. Can you drop a glass slipper at least?

JESSICA. I tried to say goodbye, you were rather surrounded.

BOB. You're really leaving now?

JESSICA. It's almost midnight.

BOB. That's kind of the point.

JESSICA. I promised my child-minder she could go to a party. She's only eighteen, you know how these things matter.

BOB. You'll miss the fireworks.

JESSICA. I'll watch from the streetcar.

BOB. I'll walk down with you, get you a cab –

JESSICA. Truly, Bob, the streetcar's fine. I like it. Anyway, I understand there's some kind of ban on Pleasure Driving.

BOB. I think you can allow yourself a little pleasure at New Year's.

JESSICA (*hard*). I've no doubt you do.

BOB. What?

JESSICA. Nothing. I'm simply agreeing.

He frowns, perplexed by her tone. They stand there awkwardly, half-wanting to escape each other, half-unable to move.

Thanks for a super evening. Do thank Ike, too, if you can disentangle him from Joyce. I'm assuming that *is* Joyce, under the piano?

BOB. That is Joyce.

JESSICA. So it worked, 'Please Come to Washington'. Do you suppose he *will* marry her?

BOB. I don't think so, no.

JESSICA. I'm glad. He'd never be faithful and she'd have a miserable life with him, so I hope she has other plans. She looks an independent sort of girl – at least she *did,* before she sank all those martinis.

BOB. Dec, has something upset you?

JESSICA. Me? Why?

BOB. Just a feeling.

JESSICA. I'm tired, that's all. I want to go home, pull the blankets over my head and for 1942 to be over. It's been a beastly year and I'm glad to see the back of it.

BOB. It wasn't all bad, was it?

JESSICA. Not all of it.

A female partygoer shouts, off: 'Hey, Treuhaft, five minutes till lift-off!' JESSICA *makes to leave.*

BOB (*grabs her hand*). Don't go.

A beat. She withdraws her hand, keeping her voice light.

JESSICA. Bob, who are all those blondes?

BOB. Blondes?

JESSICA. I was talking to them in the kitchen. Kay and Carol-Ann and Helen, and Margie with the teeth.

BOB. Kay and Helen are Harvard buddies. I wouldn't call Margie a blonde.

JESSICA. Peroxide. And Carol-Ann?

BOB. They're all good chums.

JESSICA. I gather they all got a 'Dear Joyce' record too.

BOB. Sure, I told you, didn't I? It came out so well, we switched the names, had a bunch made and sent them out to a few girlfriends as an invite to the party.

JESSICA. Well, no wonder they're all so 'full of pep', as the magazines say.

BOB. They're smart girls, they know it's in fun.

JESSICA. And is it? In fun?

BOB. Would you mind if it wasn't?

JESSICA. I? Not in the least.

BOB. Dec, help me out here –

JESSICA (*with a sudden determination*). Listen, Bob, I ought to tell you something. I'm thinking about getting transferred to San Francisco in the new year.

BOB. You're *what*?

JESSICA. More than thinking, really. I've decided. I'm not the type of girl who can stay in any place too long. Esmond and I came here to make a new life, and it turned out rather differently than we'd planned, but I think I've made the best of it, don't you? I've made great friends –

BOB. Look at me.

JESSICA (*pressing on*). Tremendous friends. But I'm ready for a change. 1943! Who knows what might happen? We might win the war, if the Soviets keep up the pressure –

BOB. Why San Francisco? It's the other side of the damn country!

JESSICA. I don't know, it has a sort of promise. Perhaps it's the Golden Gate.

BOB. You won't know a single soul.

JESSICA. Not at first, but I'll meet people. One always does, if one knows how. Besides, I have Dinky. I don't need anyone else.

Off, the countdown to New Year begins. She gives him a brilliant smile.

You'd better get back. Enjoy your party.

BOB. Enjoy it? How?

She reaches out and lightly touches his face.

JESSICA. Happy new year, Bob.

She leaves him alone. Off, cheering, and voices raised in song.

Scene Two

The schoolroom, Swinbrook, February 1937.

Bouquets of white flowers stand on every surface. DIANA *(twenty-seven) is arranging some in a vase.*

NANCY *(thirty-three) is on the telephone.*

NANCY *(into phone).* I'm sorry, neither of my parents can come to the telephone right now... I'll pass that on, of course... we so appreciate your concern. Goodbye for now, thank you –

UNITY *(twenty-three) enters with a huge bouquet of flowers.* DIANA *gestures to* NANCY.

Oh – and please don't send flowers!

NANCY *replaces the receiver. It immediately starts ringing again.* DIANA *takes the flowers from* UNITY, *who is wearing a large enamel swastika pinned to her sweater.*

DIANA. Can't they keep *some* downstairs?

UNITY. They could open a florist downstairs.

NANCY (*into phone*). Hello? No, this is Nancy, I'm afraid neither of my parents can come to the telephone… Of course, I shall. Thanks so much, we're so touched by your concern. No need to send flowers.

She replaces the receiver. UNITY *has thrown herself disconsolately into an armchair, toying with her brooch.* DIANA *is opening the card that came with the flowers.*

DIANA. 'From Lord and Lady Hulme with our deepest sympathies.' Black-edged! Someone needs to tell the press that nobody's *died*.

NANCY. People are awfully stupid, aren't they? I suppose they mean well.

DIANA. People don't know what to say.

NANCY. I wish they simply didn't *know*. Why on earth did Farve have to go to the newspapers? We could have found Decca ourselves without this absurd hullabaloo; she was bound to get in touch eventually.

DIANA. I suppose he thought publicity would help.

NANCY. Well, it's confused the issue horribly, especially for Debo.

UNITY. What do you mean, why Debo?

DIANA. The *Daily Express* mixed them up, put Debo instead of Decca, with an enormous photo too, poor lamb.

NANCY. 'Deborah Mitford, latest! Peer's Daughter Missing!', 'Peer's Daughter Elopes to Spain!'. One can't walk down the street without a shrieking newsboy brandishing a rolled-up copy of one's sister.

DIANA. It'll calm down now.

NANCY. What with you two flirting with the Führer, I'm the only Mitford girl who isn't front-page news.

DIANA. Pamela isn't. And we don't flirt – don't tease.

NANCY *glances at* UNITY, *who is in a strange reverie.*

NANCY. Telling silence from the Rhinemaiden. Miles away, in Adolf's adoring arms, no doubt.

UNITY (*surfacing*). What?

NANCY (*to* DIANA). Besides, *you* flirt with everyone, you came flirting from the womb. Even dear old Nanny Blor – one smile from baby Diana and the rest of us were eclipsed forever. She's downstairs, by the way.

DIANA. Nanny's here? Oh – I'd adore to see her…

UNITY. Why don't you go down, Honks? I'm sure Farve's forgotten he ever sent you into exile. Anyway, the worst he can do is roar at you. He roared at me at the station when he saw my swastika – I don't care.

NANCY (*to* DIANA). Why should he roar now, anyway? Decca's wiped your scandal clean off the table.

UNITY. He should count himself jolly lucky to have Kit for a son-in-law –

NANCY (*pin-sharp, to* DIANA). Son-in-law? Is he going to marry you, now he's seen off his poor wife?

UNITY. He didn't *murder* her! She had galloping peritonitis!

DIANA *concentrates intently on her flower arranging.*

NANCY (*to* DIANA). He *is,* isn't he?

DIANA. Aren't these exquisite? Lisianthus.

NANCY. That's the next headline! 'Peer's Daughter Weds Widowed Blackshirt'. I'm right, aren't I? Do admit!

UNITY. You ought to save your feverish imagination for your novels. What are you writing now, anyway? I hope you're not taking a pop at me again.

NANCY. It wasn't at you, it was at Fascism. And it was funny, wasn't it, Honks?

DIANA. Even Kit found it *hilaire.* We read it aloud in bed and he shrieked.

UNITY. He didn't get half the drubbing I did, he wasn't the main part.

NANCY. Well, if you *will* be such a little fool, rhapsodising over Hitler as if he were Clark Gable –

UNITY. Shut up, Heartless! You can't begin to know what Hitler is!

NANCY. He *looks* like a furious potato.

UNITY. He was a perfect Hon about Decca running off with Esmond. I was upset and he was sweet and calm and kind. Said he'd do his utmost to keep it out of the German press, and if there's anything he can do –

NANCY. That's settled then. *Hitler* can go and get the silly goose.

The telephone rings. NANCY *snatches it up irritably.*

Yes?… No, it's Nancy… Oh – Winston! Of course, one moment –

She turns to UNITY, *covers the mouthpiece.*

Run down and tell Farve it's Churchill. Quickly!

UNITY *heaves herself up and slouches out.* NANCY *speaks into the phone.*

Is there any news at your end?… No, nothing more since Decca spoke to Muv. I gather they're determined to be married… I'm sure he *is,* a very honourable boy.

The phone is picked up at the other end.)

Oh – goodbye!

She listens briefly, then replaces the receiver.

Well, *he* might have some influence over his horrid nephew.

DIANA. Esmond Romilly is an anarchist and a Bolshevik. I don't suppose a stern word from Uncle Winston will bring him home. Last week in the House, Winston said he'd vote Hitler over the Communists.

NANCY. More fool him. Your Hitler's a menace.

DIANA. Really, dear, you don't know anything about it.

NANCY. I know enough.

DIANA. Don't be beastly to Unity, at least. She's rather fragile.

NANCY. *Unity?*

DIANA. Inside, I mean. Sometimes she says the most alarming things.

NANCY. I've heard her!

DIANA. No – I mean – when anyone suggests there could be another war. She says she couldn't bear it, to be forced to choose between England and –

She breaks off as DEBO (*seventeen*) *enters, sagging theatrically under another bouquet, followed by* UNITY.

DEBO. Golly, it's dismal down there! Muv can't stop crying, her nose has swelled up something frightful. She's sitting in a sea of lilies clutching an ancient photo of Decca, and Farve is cooking up a mad plan with Winston about sending a naval destroyer to fetch her.

NANCY. A *naval destroyer*?

UNITY (*to* NANCY). He says you or I have to go too. Honks is too sinful and Debo hasn't evolved yet. It had better be you, I'm not much use.

DEBO. I *have* evolved! I was the calmest person downstairs by a country mile. Nanny Blor's crying too, she keeps on and on about how Decca didn't pack enough knickers and hasn't the right clothes to fight in. I said, 'Nanny dear, I doubt she'll actually be in mortal combat'. (*Seized by sudden worry.*) I say, do you suppose she *will* be in mortal combat?

DIANA. No, angel. Remember what Decca said to Muv on the telephone, they're miles and miles from any actual fighting.

DEBO. But do you think that's true?

UNITY (*hotly*). Of course! Decca never lies!

NANCY. Are you mad? She *lied* that she was in Paris with the Paget twins, when actually she was halfway to Spain with that blockheaded boy!

UNITY. She wouldn't have bolted if she hadn't felt desperate.

DEBO. I think it's romantic to fall in love and run away. I didn't even care when the *Express* thought it was me – it was thrilling. (*Tears springing.*) I just don't see why she didn't tell me. I'd not have breathed a word.

NANCY. Well, she didn't and that's that. The point is, how to get her back. (*To* UNITY.) I'm willing to go if you refuse. Peter might come with me.

UNITY. I didn't refuse.

DIANA (*to* NANCY). I hope he does; one rather needs a husband in a war zone.

NANCY. He can hardly say no, he's not exactly busy. Living off my earnings and sitting about all day eating nuts.

UNITY. I'm not refusing. I just think I'm the last person.

DIANA. You're her best Boud. Her partner-in-crime.

UNITY. Not any more. She wouldn't listen to a word I say.

DEBO. Of course she would! And it might patch everything up. You might get on famously with Esmond, and Decca might feel jollier about Hitler.

UNITY. I don't see why I *shouldn't* get along with Esmond. Naturally, if it came to it, I'd shoot him, but till then we might as well be chums.

NANCY. Shoot him?

UNITY. Crack! Right through the cranium!

NANCY (*decisively*). Peter and I will go to Spain, with the entire Royal Navy if necessary. I'll go and tell Farve.

She sweeps out. DEBO *gazes wistfully after her.*

DEBO. I wish I could go. Do you suppose Farve would let me?

DIANA. No, dear.

DEBO. Why? I'd be with Naunce and boring old Peter, wouldn't I? I should so love to see Decca get married. I shall ask. Naunce, wait for me!

She runs out. DIANA *and* UNITY *are left alone.* UNITY *fiddles with the flowers.*

UNITY (*softly*). Loves me... loves me not...

DIANA. Don't pluck them, darling, they'll die.

UNITY. I'm not. Only the leaves, not the petals.

A beat. She glances around to ensure they're alone.

Honks, do forgive!

DIANA. What for, silly girl?

UNITY. You and Kit getting married; I almost spilled the beans.

DIANA. Oh, don't worry about that. I shall 'fess up soon. I'll wait till I'm *in pig,* then I'll tell them. Wouldn't want Muv to think I'm spawning piglets out of wedlock.

UNITY. It was the most divine day. I shall remember it all my life.

DIANA. When you and I were dressing, and I looked out and saw Hitler crossing the lawn with his wedding gift – I thought: I'll never know such perfect happiness. Darling Goebbels and Magda were so sweet to lend us their home and make such an occasion of it. Kit and I felt blessed by the angels. (*Warmly.*) You'll be next.

UNITY. No, I don't think so.

DIANA. Someone heroic will snap you up.

She looks over at her with a smile, then shivers.

What is it, darling? Don't look like that, it frightens me.

UNITY. I just have this queer feeling everything's drawing to a close.

DIANA (*urgently*). But you mustn't feel like that, you *mustn't* – there's no need! Everything's just beginning! No one wants another war. Hitler cares a very great deal for this country, and even more for you. And Decca will come home, and –

UNITY. Honks, when you last saw him – Hitler – did you meet Miss Braun?

DIANA. The girl who takes the pictures?

UNITY. Eva. Do you think she's pretty?

DIANA. Not bad. She'll run to fat, I expect.

UNITY. People are saying she's his mistress.

A beat.

DIANA. It's possible. Would you mind awfully, dear?

UNITY (*a desperate bravado*). How could I mind? I haven't any claim on him at all. I *want* him to be happy. I wondered what she looks like, that's all.

Scene Three

Nancy's bedroom. France, 1969.

NANCY (*sixty-five*) *sits on the edge of the bed, grey-faced, a heap of shopping bags and parcels at her feet.* JESSICA (*fifty-three*) *enters with a bouquet of roses.*

JESSICA. How are you feeling? You're a slightly better colour.

NANCY. Who sent those?

JESSICA. They were in the porch, the taxi driver spotted them.

NANCY. Did you tip him?

JESSICA. Yes, of course.

NANCY. You shouldn't have; it's an insult in France. Although wasn't he kind to drive so slowly? Most of the cab men in Paris are simply lunatics.

JESSICA. I think he'd half a mind to take us straight to the hospital. And I'm not sure we shouldn't have gone.

NANCY. Don't be so dramatic, it was a funny turn, that's all. I'm perfectly fine. And weren't we lucky to run into Honks!

JESSICA makes a small indecipherable sound.

One might have guessed she'd be there of course. Wouldn't miss a designer sale if it killed her. Where is she?

JESSICA. Making tea, I believe.

NANCY. Is the girl not here?

JESSICA. Day off, remember? (*Re: the roses.*) Are they from your Colonel?

NANCY. He can be awfully spoiling when he knows he's in disgrace. It makes it rather difficult to stay cross with him, but –

She has opened the card. A beat; lightly:

They're for you.

JESSICA. Me?

NANCY. Not a special birthday, is it?

JESSICA. Fifty-three.

NANCY. Hardly a milestone.

JESSICA. Not at all.

NANCY. How wildly romantic, to send all the way to France. What an extravagant chap you married.

She shoves the flowers back at JESSICA.

Best put them in water, they're not the sort that lasts.

JESSICA. Don't you want to get into your nightclothes?

NANCY. I shan't sleep, I'll just rest for a moment.

JESSICA. Let's jettison the coat and shoes at least, shall we?

NANCY. I can manage, Decca. There's a vase in my dressing room.

JESSICA *obediently exits with the roses. Left alone,* NANCY *briefly succumbs to her pain and unhappiness. She covers it, brightly, as* JESSICA *returns with a vase.*

Was that the only one?

JESSICA. Yes, won't it do?

NANCY (*laughs*). Poor old Dec, you look done-in. Was it a frightful shock?

JESSICA. (*grateful*) It was, rather. Debo did say that you sometimes –

NANCY. Seeing Honks, I mean.

JESSICA *stares at her.* NANCY *continues, warming to her theme.*

She's aged terribly well, do admit. She could be ten years younger. Rather like the French girls – she doesn't fight it. Let her hair go that marvellous silver, kept her figure naturally with all that tennis and sailing and walking. Of course, the eyes are as *extrorder* as ever.

JESSICA. I didn't really think about Diana. I was too concerned about you.

She crams the roses into the too-small vase. NANCY *observes her maliciously.*

NANCY. She's turned into quite a surprising person, as it happens. One never really thought of her as a brain, but that's what she's become. Reads everything, sees everything. Can't be outdone on current affairs.

JESSICA *snorts.*

I've always rather wondered why you blame her so.

JESSICA. Let's not talk about it now.

NANCY. You don't think she served her time? Four years in that foul prison, torn away from the babies –

JESSICA. I'm sure it wasn't very pleasant.

NANCY. Pleasant? I should say not! Filthy conditions, dysentery, and the *food,* positively crawling with –

JESSICA. She'll come in, can't we leave it, please?

NANCY. I'm merely asking, wasn't that enough for you?

JESSICA. Naunce, you said when I arrived, let's not dwell on the past. (*Firmly, before* NANCY *can interrupt.*) And I think you were absolutely right.

A beat. NANCY *turns the little Interflora card in her fingers.*

NANCY. Everyone's been marvelling at my garden for weeks. The doctor, the postman… that parched little woman from the literary society who talked and talked until I thought I'd die of listening. 'How beautiful your roses are, Miss Mitford. Just like the ones Fabrice gives to Linda in *The Pursuit of Love.*' But it never occurred to a single soul to bring some in so that I might enjoy them too.

JESSICA. Well, *these* are yours now. From me.

NANCY. But why must one be forced to spell everything out? Why isn't there a person on *earth* who can anticipate one's needs? Who can look at one and *know,* without being told, what would make one better? Only the Colonel did, you see. From the very first, he knew – how to make me laugh, to feel desired, adored… And Nanny Blor, when I was little. Nanny knew. Before the rest of you pitched up and ruined everything.

JESSICA. Try not to upset yourself; it won't help the pain.

NANCY. Nothing helps the pain, that's the trouble. If painkillers won't kill it, I shall simply have to accept it as my lot. And it isn't fair.

JESSICA. I know it isn't, darling.

NANCY (*a flash of rage*). You *don't* know, how could you possibly? You don't know anything at all. You can't even arrange a vase of flowers. Really, Decca, how entirely

ACT TWO, SCENE THREE 69

lacking in grace your life must be if you could make something so beautiful look so primitive and tasteless!

JESSICA *moves swiftly away, draws out* DEBO*'s notes.* NANCY *watches, briefly contrite.*

I'm not saying you haven't suffered. Of course you have.

JESSICA *picks up the telephone.*

What are you doing?

JESSICA. One of these endless doctors ought to check you over.

NANCY. Don't call anyone. Please. There isn't any need.

JESSICA. You just said yourself –

NANCY. But I'm fine now! Look at me, it passes! Rather galling, since the dreaded Lumpular was entirely sliced out – but one must expect a bit of pain, after surgery.

JESSICA (*carefully*). Still, worth a touch more investigation, wouldn't you say? Not today – I mean, at some point?

NANCY. Darling, I've been more thoroughly investigated than you and your Commie comrades. Lumpular has been asked 'Are you now or have you ever been?' and it said firmly, 'No.'

JESSICA. One can't have too many second opinions.

NANCY. In fact, one *can*. Stop fretting, it's terribly tiresome.

JESSICA *glances towards the door.*

JESSICA. Naunce, listen. If it were me –

NANCY. Yes, I'm beginning to think you *should* see a doctor. You look like you've swallowed a pinecone, what on earth is the matter?

A beat. JESSICA *can't say what she wants to say.*

JESSICA. I feel responsible. It was too much for you today.

NANCY. Well, don't. It was my idea and I'm glad we did it. I've been cooped up long enough. Besides, think of all your lovely new clothes.

JESSICA. I can't think how you convinced me. Dear God, all that *money*.

NANCY. For heaven's sake, Decca, you're rich! You never tire of telling us all how successful you are – why don't you dress like it? What are you saving up for, going about like a dowdy housewife in a cornflake commercial? What's it *for,* if one can't get a little pleasure from it?

JESSICA. Talk about pot and kettle! You're the meanest old skinflint I ever met.

NANCY. Not when it comes to clothes.

JESSICA. I never got much pleasure from that. I always found it absurd.

NANCY. Nonsense. You don't remember. When Peter and I came out to Spain to try and drag you home, I brought a stack of *Vogue* magazines and –

JESSICA. I do remember, actually.

NANCY. On and on you talked about the poor refugees, the women feeding newborns under their jerseys, the huge eyes of the little starving children – then out came a few back copies of *Vogue* and you practically swallowed them whole. Never mind General Franco, all of a sudden –

JESSICA. One has nothing to do with the other!

NANCY. I happen to think it does! Why begrudge oneself? You look *wondair* in that outfit, it takes ten years off you, not to mention half a stone.

JESSICA. And half my earnings for the year.

NANCY. Good clothes cost money, that's all there is to it. You make countless public appearances; I can't imagine you go about dressed like *this*.

ACT TWO, SCENE THREE   71

JESSICA. Of course not, I've plenty of decent clothes.

NANCY. A Dior jacket will last your entire life, and let's face it, you're more than halfway through. And at that price you were fearfully lucky. Debo spends three times that at Dior in London.

JESSICA (*exhausted*). Won't you try to rest a little, Naunce?

NANCY. Besides, it's your birthday present.

JESSICA. To myself?

NANCY. Why not? I haven't exactly thrown you a party.

JESSICA. I don't care about that sort of thing.

NANCY. One has to reward oneself for one's survival, don't you think?

DIANA (*fifty-nine*) *enters with a tray of tea. Despite the assumption of normality, between she and* JESSICA *there is a heightened awareness of each other's presence; perhaps avoiding direct eye contact, or conscious of making it. She puts down the tea, assessing* NANCY.

DIANA. You look rather brighter.

NANCY. More than one can say for Decca. She's reeling because I made her dip into her vast fortune.

JESSICA. If I'm reeling it's because you collapsed in the street like a sack of King Edwards.

NANCY. Honks, tell her, won't you? I'm perfectly fine now.

DIANA. Did you take a pink pill?

NANCY. I don't need a pink pill. I want to work this afternoon.

JESSICA. I think she ought to rest.

NANCY. I'm afraid our Decca's become terribly straitlaced and querulous in her old age. (*To* JESSICA.) You're supposed to be the rebel – the *mouton noir*. You ought to be encouraging me to go out dancing.

DIANA. I agree with Decca. You need a pink pill and an afternoon in bed.

NANCY. Well, you're frightful bores, the pair of you. My darling Fred the Great is waiting patiently in my study; I shall rest for an hour and then join him there. And no ghastly brain-numbing pills to ruin our *rendezvous.* That's my last word. Decca, show Honks what you bought.

JESSICA. What?

NANCY. Let's have a fashion show.

JESSICA. Absolutely not.

NANCY. Oh, be a Hon! (*To* DIANA.) She looks *wondair* in the suit, it makes the most tremendous difference. When something's been properly cut, you see. (*To* JESSICA.) Go on. You can use my dressing room.

DIANA. Don't be a bully. If she doesn't want to –

JESSICA. All right, I'll do it.

NANCY (*to* DIANA). There, you see. (*To* JESSICA.) And don't judge anything in there, it's the worst mirror in the house.

JESSICA *picks up her parcels and exits.* DIANA *pours tea, her back to* NANCY.

Are you laughing?

DIANA. 'A fashion show'.

NANCY. It's for her own good.

DIANA. You're absolute evil.

NANCY. You don't know the half.

DIANA *brings over her tea. They sip in silence for a moment, quietly amused.*

Anyway, she does look jolly nice in it. It was a bargain, and nothing could be worse than that mannish shirt and awful 'slacks'. All very well in one's own home, but what does she wear when she's eviscerating capitalism on the *Today* show –

DIANA (*laughing*). Shh…

NANCY. Or swanning around Hollywood? Every time she thunderously drops a name – 'Julie Andrews says my memoir simply *has* to be a film', 'Vanessa Redgrave said at lunch that she'd die to play Unity' – all I can think is, but darling, what were you wearing?

DIANA. I suppose one never quite knows what suits one.

NANCY. Don't be saintly. *You* do. I do! Mark my words, she'll come out in that divinely chic outfit saying she loathes it all. The wool itches, the blouse is too tight and it's all going back tomorrow. That's Decca. She won't let herself have it.

JESSICA emerges from the dressing room. She wears a Dior jacket, blouse and skirt, beautifully cut and flattering. It's quite a transformation. NANCY *sits up, triumphant.*

JESSICA glances instinctively at DIANA, *who wears a serene, non-committal smile.*

NANCY. Well, you *may* go to the ball!

JESSICA. I'm not at all sure.

NANCY (*to* DIANA). What did I just say?

JESSICA. I ought to have gone a size up in the blouse.

NANCY. Not a bit, it's wonderfully slimming. Better than all those flannel shirts that make you look like the Himalayas. Where are the shoes?

JESSICA (*gestures*). In there.

NANCY. Put them on.

JESSICA. Must I? Now?

NANCY. Or it's half an outfit.

With a sigh, JESSICA *removes the shoes from their box and slips them on.*

The shoes were a snip. See why she had to have them?

JESSICA. The left one pinches, it didn't in the shop.

NANCY. Walk about a bit. Undo the jacket. (*To* DIANA.) The colour's a triumph – brings out her eyes.

DIANA, smiling, says nothing. JESSICA *turns away from their scrutiny, pours a cup of tea.*

JESSICA. I was in New York last week with Judy Garland –

NANCY *and* DIANA *exchange a tiny glance, maybe stifle a giggle.*

And we happened to walk past a dress store where I used to work, when Esmond and I first moved there. 'Jane Engels of Madison Ave'. When we hadn't a cent between us and had to take on all sorts of jobs. I'd quite forgotten but it all came flooding back. How I'd turned out to be rather good at it; made a vast commission, convincing rich ladies to buy terrifically expensive clothes that looked frightful on them.

NANCY. You don't look a bit frightful. I'd be the first to tell you.

JESSICA. It's surprisingly easy. People just want to be flattered.

NANCY. Well, what's in it for us? We don't get any commission at all. Don't wave that cup about, you'll spill – and look in the mirror, you need to see the whole ensemble.

JESSICA. I saw it in the dressing room.

NANCY. I told you, you can't judge in there.

JESSICA. The collar's awfully scratchy –

Without warning, DIANA *gently takes her by the shoulders and turns her to the mirror.*

JESSICA *catches her breath.*

DIANA (*softly*). Wait.

She slips off her own necklace and puts it around JESSICA*'s neck, lifting her hair to fasten the catch. As she does this, there's a sudden sense of* UNITY *in the room – a rustle, a glimpse in the mirror, or in* JESSICA*'s line of vision.* JESSICA *jerks wildly away from* DIANA.

JESSICA. No – it's no good, it has to go back!

NANCY. Have you lost your mind?

JESSICA. I don't want it. It has to go back.

Scene Four

The Englischer Garten, Munich, Germany. September 1939.

UNITY (*twenty-five*) *sits on a park bench reading a newspaper. The front page announces: 'DER KRIEG MIT ENGLAND'.* UNITY *lowers the newspaper, a little half-smile on her face.*

A voice, off, calls out in friendly greeting, 'Guten Morgen, Fräulein!'

UNITY (*calls off, brightly*). *Was für ein wonderschöner Tag!*

She waits for the person to disappear, then folds the newspaper with care and places it on the bench beside her. She takes off her reading glasses and puts them on top. She takes a small revolver from her bag and raises it to her temple. Closes her eyes and –

Scene Five

The Office of Price Adminstration, Washington, 1943. Early afternoon.

BOB *sits at his desk, where he has set up a DIY phonograph. He is picking lightly on a ukulele. He clears his throat and sings to the tune of the 'Dear Joyce' song:*

BOB (*sings*).
Dear Dec, come back to Washington, before I turn to drink,
Please come back before they have to throw me in the clink,

76   THE PARTY GIRLS

Come home and join the Reds with me and be my ballroom
  pink,
Dear Dec, come back and marry me – I miss you and the
  Dink!

*He plays it back, pleased with his handiwork, then takes
the record off the turntable and polishes it carefully with
a duster. He picks up the telephone.*

(*Into phone.*) Office of Price Administration, San Francisco,
please...

Hello, this is Bob Treuhaft from the Washington office, may
I speak with Decca Romilly?... Sure, I'll hold. But listen –
can you tell her its Boris Karloff?... You know the actor,
Boris Karloff?... Frankenstein's monster?... No?... Well,
can you tell her anyway? Tell her Boris Karloff wants to take
her Pleasure Driving... No, it's a joke... Yes, I'm confident
she'll find it funny... That's right, Boris Karloff. Thank you.

He waits. His face lights up.

Hey, how'd you guess? I *knew* you'd pick up for Boris.
When it's plain old Bob you always seem to be out of the
office... You do? Right this minute?... Listen, it's fine.
Another time... Sure we will. Boris Karloff is kind of busy
too, as it happens. Up to his neck-bolts in – in all sorts of
business. You bet. You take care, Dauntless.

*He puts down the phone, is still for a beat. Puts the record
over his knee, and breaks it in half.*

Scene Six

Nancy's bedroom, France, 1969.

JESSICA (*fifty-three*) *is changing back into her old clothes;
half-Dior, half 'housewife from a cornflake commercial'. As
she takes off each item of the Dior suit, she folds it tenderly,*

ACT TWO, SCENE SIX 77

regretfully back into its tissue wrapping. DIANA *(fifty-nine) appears, startling her.*

JESSICA. One moment, let me just –

DIANA. I can come back in a tick.

JESSICA. It's all right –

She pulls her old sweater over her head, emerging.

There. Am I needed?

DIANA. I came to say goodbye, actually. She's ensconced in her study with Fred the Great and a roaring fire, and a very small Glenlivet. She seems fine. Do ring up, if not.

JESSICA. Thanks for doing all that.

DIANA. My pleasure.

JESSICA. I expect you're rather better at it than me. I get on her nerves.

DIANA. You must ignore her when she gets like that, she doesn't mean it.

JESSICA. Naunce always means it; she always did.

DIANA. But it's different now. It's the pain – and the effort of trying to hide it. Poor darling Naunce – isn't it the worst?

Her eyes are full of tears. She takes out a handkerchief and dabs at them. JESSICA *looks away, fusses with the bedspread.*

JESSICA. Does anyone ever plan to tell her the truth?

DIANA. I'm not sure we *know* the truth. None of the specialists can agree.

JESSICA. But the prognosis is bad. That's what Debo said. And I personally think it would be better for her to know *now,* whilst she's at least *physically* strong enough to bear it.

DIANA. She has to finish Fred the Great.

JESSICA. Why, for pity's sake? If I were that unwell, I'd hope my publisher –

DIANA (*sharply*). Because that's how Naunce makes sense of her life. She hasn't the solace of husbands and children as we do; even the Colonel's gone. And to write the way she does – she must have hope. Do you see? She must have light. I think to take that away from her now would be –

JESSICA. Fatal?

DIANA. I do, as it happens.

JESSICA. And I suppose what I think doesn't matter.

DIANA. You see, the rest of us have been here.

> JESSICA *nods. A beat.*

I gather you've joined the grandma club. Isn't it marvellous?

JESSICA. Isn't it.

DIANA. Has he a name?

JESSICA. The baby? James, after his father.

She looks steadily at DIANA.

Dinky's chap is African-American. He's a tremendous force in civil rights at the moment, really the go-to man. The Dink's very happy. As are we. We like him awfully. A great deal of our work is in race relations so –

DIANA. And I expect baby's enchanting.

JESSICA. He is.

A beat.

DIANA. I must make a move. It's been *wondair* to see you after all this time, you haven't changed a bit. What a stroke of good luck to be in Paris today.

JESSICA. Surely Naunce set it up.

DIANA. Well, I hadn't a clue.

JESSICA. She was awfully determined to get to Dior.

DIANA. I'm glad, at any rate. I hope we shall see each other again.

ACT TWO, SCENE SIX

She holds out a hand. JESSICA *hesitates.*

We're getting rather ancient, Decca. Mightn't we be friends?

JESSICA (*slowly, almost entranced*). It's funny. When we stood by that mirror, I could almost have forgiven you anything. Never mind the poison you brought into our home. Never mind Unity, how you controlled her –

DIANA. *I?* Controlled *Unity?*

JESSICA. Utterly, yes, of course you did, but never mind that. Never mind the war and everyone it swallowed up – our friends, our brother. *Esmond.* Never mind everything I've fought for and campaigned against, all my life. Suddenly nothing mattered except your approval. Whether you liked me. Whether you thought I looked pretty.

DIANA. I *never* withdrew my approval. You withdrew yours!

JESSICA. And why do you suppose that was?

DIANA. Good heavens, am I on trial again?

JESSICA. You're free to leave at any time.

DIANA. What is it, exactly, that you want from me?

JESSICA. I want you to *admit,* Diana! *Do admit!*

They stare at each other, finally face to face.

Why can't you say it? For twenty *years* I've watched you being interviewed, read countless profiles: 'Lady Mosley at Home'. I'm always waiting for the moment, and it never comes. You still defend him. And I don't mean your husband, monstrous as he is –

DIANA. You don't know Kit, you never tried.

JESSICA. I said I *don't* mean him.

DIANA. It isn't fair to –

JESSICA. Fair? What's *fair*? To erase from the earth six million people for nothing – *nothing* – for being who they are? Admit it isn't. Admit it makes no odds how clever or charming he was – that he kissed your hand – he liked

Tristan and Isolde – he had terrific table manners! Admit you threw in your lot with the Devil – yes, the Devil – and don't say Stalin was worse – just say it! Be as good as you *are*! Be better!

A beat. DIANA *takes a pair of driving gloves from her pocket and draws them on.*

DIANA (*lightly*). One can't help wondering why you're all so fixed on that number.

JESSICA. What number?

DIANA. Why must it always be 'six million'?

JESSICA. Because it *was*! At the very least!

DIANA. Yes, I'm afraid I can't quite believe that.

JESSICA. You think it's a *lie*?

DIANA. I'd call it an exaggeration. 'Six million' sounds more dramatic than one, two. 'Six million' will hold the world to ransom for a very long time.

JESSICA. I don't understand. What are you saying?

DIANA. Simply that it's going to be the most enormous industry. I've been reading all about it; it's only just beginning, now the survivors are starting to talk. And why shouldn't they, poor souls? But once the floodgates are open... You wait. Books and films and documentaries, acres of barbed wire and cattle trucks. We're going to have to sit through an awful lot of that.

JESSICA (*through gritted teeth*). So we should. Over and over. Never enough.

DIANA. Yes, dear... but there will come a time when people *have* had enough. There always does, in the end. Then Hitler and his achievements might be seen in quite a different light. We shan't be here to witness it, alas.

She moves to exit, then turns, with a warm smile.

You did look smashing in that outfit. I'd hold on to it if I were you.

Scene Seven

The schoolroom, Swinbrook, 1940.

UNITY (*twenty-five*) *is sitting at the table, doing a child's jigsaw puzzle and sloppily eating a bowl of soup. She wears a large dirty bandage wrapped around her head and her expression is childlike and blank. The sleeves of her cardigan trail in the soup. She breathes heavily through her nose as she concentrates on the puzzle.* DEBO (*twenty*) *sits nearby, knitting a scarf.*

UNITY. Stop clicking.

DEBO. What?

UNITY. Your needles make a click-click sound. It gives me a pain.

DEBO. Sorry.

She tries to knit silently.

UNITY. I can still hear it.

DEBO. Well, I can hear you slurping like a spaniel.

She throws the knitting aside and picks up a magazine, flips through it listlessly. UNITY *stirs her jigsaw pieces, searching for something.* DEBO *tries for brightness.*

They've added Vitamin A to Pond's Cold Cream, we ought to try it. (*Reads.*) 'The Lady Alexandra Haig, who often sings at charity events, says she feels even more enthusiastic about using it.'

UNITY. I've a piece missing.

DEBO. Oh dear. Shall I help you look?

UNITY. I think you took it?

DEBO. Me?

UNITY. It's the top of the snake's head and a bit of grass.

DEBO. I didn't take it. What on earth would I want with it?

UNITY. I'm going to tell Muv.

DEBO. You can broadcast it on the Home Service for all I care.

UNITY (*standing*). Give it back!

DEBO. Oh, leave me alone, why don't you? I haven't got your hateful snake's head or any bit of your stupid puzzle! It's probably in the box.

UNITY. It isn't – you took it! You took it!

She picks up the jigsaw box and pitches the contents at DEBO, *who ducks with a scream as* NANCY (*thirty-five*) *enters, smartly dressed and made-up, with a glittering energy about her.*

DEBO. Naunce, you darling, oh you Hon! Am I glad to see *you*! It's been absolute hell! I've been cooped up alone, for days – with *her* – and it's perfectly dismal! Muv and Farve are barely on speakers –

NANCY. Where are they? (*To* UNITY.) Hello, dear.

UNITY. She took my snake's head. She's got it and she won't give it back.

NANCY. Snake's head?

DEBO. She keeps saying that, ignore her. Farve's in town at his club, didn't he tell you? And Muv's with Pam for a few days. She's been doing simply everything, including washing *her* sheets and underwear twice a day. She won't let anyone help. Farve's no use, he can hardly look at her –

NANCY (*considering* UNITY). Small wonder. One could wring another bowl of soup from those sleeves, dear. Any thoughts about rolling them up?

UNITY *ignores her, continues stolidly eating her soup.*

She looks better than last time.

DEBO. Oh she is, physically! But I think in *here* – (*She taps her head.*) it's worse. Farve's convinced the German doctors caused a bleed when they tried to move the bullet. Or the bullet's pressing on some crucial bit of brain. She didn't blink when Kit was arrested. She doesn't even react if one mentions Hitler. (*Louder.*) Adolf Hitler.

UNITY *is oblivious, continues eating.*

NANCY. She can't have forgotten.

DEBO. She forgets everything. She'll have forgotten in five seconds about the wretched snake.

UNITY. No I won't.

DEBO. Won't what?

UNITY *stares at her with hatred.* DEBO *gestures to* NANCY.

See? You can tell her anything, it goes straight out of her head. She asks the same questions over and over: 'Where's Decca, where's Muv, what's for lunch?' – while she's actually *eating* it! And I'm horrid to her – no, I *am,* and I hate myself for it – but sometimes it's hard to be patient and kind when it feels like one's life is suspended and everything bright and hopeful and true is happening elsewhere! Oh Naunce, I'm babbling, aren't I? It's because I'm so happy to see you.

She suddenly, fully takes NANCY *in.*

You look nice. Have you been somewhere snazzy?

NANCY. Hardly. The Muse has abandoned me, and I'm not on blackout duty, Peter's not at home – not *our* home, anyway – so I thought I'd come out and relieve you. Do you want to go up to town, stay at the flat?

DEBO *gazes at her, hope dawning in her eyes.*

DEBO. Is this a tease?

NANCY. No, silly child, I'm here, aren't I?

DEBO. But – do you mean it, really?

NANCY (*crossing her heart*). Hope to die.

DEBO. Oh, you heavenly Hon! If I ever again, in the whole of our lives, cast any aspersion on your Honnishness, remind me of this moment?

NANCY. Yes, yes…

DEBO. I shall adore you mercilessly for ever! Do you mind if I go somewhere quiet and make some telephone calls, see if anyone's about?

NANCY. Not in the least.

DEBO. Naunce, you're a saint, a saint!

NANCY. Go, before I change my mind!

DEBO kisses her and flies out. Then flies immediately back in again, grabs NANCY's hands.

DEBO. You see, there might be someone. A chap. I don't know yet, but there might be. I mean, there *is,* he does exist. I haven't made him up.

NANCY. Darling, how wonderful; who?

DEBO. Andrew Cavendish. He's awfully nice. We met at a supper party and then he invited a gang of us to the family pile –

NANCY. Chatsworth?

DEBO. Yes, and it was glorious fun, and rather serious too – (*She claps a hand to her heart.*) you know, a thunderbolt! And he's about to join up, and I thought I wouldn't see him, but because you're such a saint – why, your hands, they're shaking –

NANCY. I shall have to get into the airing cupboard. Run along now.

DEBO kisses her again and runs out. NANCY watches her go.

Good old Debo. 'Marry a duke.' Perhaps she will.

UNITY. I don't think you're a saint.

NANCY. Why do you say that?

UNITY. I don't think you are.

A beat.

NANCY. Well, you're right. I'm not.

UNITY *concentrates hard on her jigsaw puzzle.*

I went to Whitehall this morning. To talk about Honks.

Still focussed on her jigsaw, UNITY *starts humming, softly at first, but growing louder.*

He was charming, the MI5 chap. Said his wife reads all my books. And frankly, there was nothing I could tell him that he didn't know already. He's been watching Honks for years and years. He knows she's hand-in-glove with Hitler and went countless times to Germany before the War. He knows she leaked all sorts of information to the Nazis, and he knows she's still on speakers with Hitler now. He had the most enormous dossier – (*Sharply.*) Stop humming!

UNITY *is still and silent in her chair, eyes fixed on the floor.*

He only really wanted confirmation. All I had to do was nod my head. I said: 'You do realise she has four children? The baby is only a few weeks old.' He said he's not in the habit of locking up young mothers, but this is an exceptional case. Diana Mosley is an exceptionally dangerous person. And I said: yes. She is.

A beat.

Say something.

UNITY. There it is.

NANCY. What?

UNITY. My missing piece.

UNITY *crouches, picks up a jigsaw piece from the floor and gazes at it, turning it over and over as though she doesn't know what to do with it.* NANCY *watches her, troubled.*

Where's Decca?

NANCY. Decca's in America, darling. That's where she lives.

UNITY. America! Is she happy?

NANCY. I don't think anyone's terribly happy at the moment.

UNITY. But do you think she might be, one day?

NANCY stares at her blankly.

NANCY. I haven't the least idea.

Scene Eight

San Francisco, 1943. The fire escape outside Jessica's apartment. A warm September evening, the sun just starting to set.

BOB (*thirty-one*) *is perched on the fire escape landing, a small suitcase beside him.* JESSICA (*twenty-six*) *appears at the open window. She speaks in a loud whisper, which he unconsciously imitates.*

JESSICA. Here, Bob – take this –

She passes him a picnic hamper, followed by other accoutrements.

Wait, and this –

BOB. Why are we whispering?

JESSICA. It's Dinky, she's asleep!

She clambers out to join him and shuts the window. Now they can stop whispering.

BOB. This is genuinely the best way in and out of your apartment?

JESSICA. One gets used to it. Of course, the other way is through the house, but my landlady isn't home and the Marines are at their tango class.

BOB. The Marines?

JESSICA. The boys downstairs, you'll adore them.

BOB. The boys downstairs, hey?

JESSICA. They can't wait to meet you.

They smile at each other. A beat.

BOB. You look terrific, Dauntless.

JESSICA. I feel terrific, as it happens.

BOB. Well, you look it.

She flings open the hamper and busies herself with its contents.

JESSICA. Yes, the Dink's out cold so we ought to make the most of tonight – catch up on each other's news, that is! How far's your hotel?

BOB. Just a block downtown.

JESSICA. Splendid! If you don't mind having supper out here –

BOB. It's a beautiful evening.

JESSICA. It's rather a scratch meal, but I can offer you cold beer, cold chicken, potato salad and peaches – fresh, not canned. You'll notice I say 'canned' now rather than 'tinned', which makes me more or less a US citizen, wouldn't you say? And finally, the *piéce de resistance* – just to say: you're a splendid pal to come all this way to see us.

She hands him a small cake tin.

It won't be a patch on your mother's. I had to use raspberry jam instead of apricot which felt faintly criminal.

BOB. You're kidding…

JESSICA. I'm afraid not. It seems there's an apricot drought in San Francisco.

BOB. You made *rigó jancsi*?

JESSICA. Are you ravenous? You must be, after all that travelling.

He gently puts down the box.

BOB. I'm not in a rush.

JESSICA. Perhaps we'll wait a bit.

BOB (*simultaneous*). Decca, listen –

JESSICA (*simultaneous*). Have you seen –

A beat of shared laughter.

BOB. You first.

JESSICA. I was going to ask if you've seen *Mission to Moscow*. I thought you might have gone with one of your blondes.

BOB. Not yet. They all seem so tied up.

JESSICA. That's the way with blondes. I've been dying to see it – all my union chums say its marvellously Pro-Soviet and true to the book. So today, when the Dink was at nursery, I thought: what the hell. One doesn't turn twenty-six every day so I skived off work, bought an immense carton of popcorn and sat through the whole movie twice.

BOB. That good?

JESSICA. Well, that's the mystery – I've no idea. I couldn't tell you a single thing about it. I didn't even notice the reel begin again. I was hoping you might be able to tell me what I missed.

BOB. From my trip with the blonde?

JESSICA. If she wasn't too distracting.

BOB. You do know, by the way, that there aren't any blondes?

JESSICA (*lightly*). None at all?

BOB. Never were.

JESSICA. Never?

BOB. Okay, once or twice –

JESSICA. I knew it! Carol-Ann!

BOB. Not after I met you.

JESSICA leaps abruptly to her feet.

Where are you going?

JESSICA. I forgot, I've some pickles too. Proper New York pickles, I mean, not actually *from* New York, but San Francisco New York pickles –

BOB. Hold it there, Dauntless. We don't need pickles. I mean – not at this moment, we don't.

JESSICA (*afraid*). Why don't we need pickles?

BOB. Because I've watched you run out on me too many times. With all kinds of reasons but it's always the same – there's a moment – and I step towards you – and you're gone. And I need to know. Are you running away from *me* – in which case, tell me, and I swear, I'll disappear –

JESSICA. Don't say that.

BOB. Or is it because you're afraid to love, or afraid of being hurt, or there's another guy, or maybe it's still Esmond. But you have to tell me. Because I think we could have a terrific life together. And I happen to believe we could do an awful lot of good.

JESSICA. Dear Bob…

BOB. Come on, hit me, I can take it. But I can't take *not knowing.* Trying to get you on the telephone, waiting for your letters. Not any more.

In the silence that follows, NANCY, DIANA, DEBO *and* UNITY *seem to appear, observing with interest, like chaperones at a ball.* JESSICA *speaks with great difficulty.*

JESSICA. I'm not who you think I am. I'm not a good person.

BOB. What do you mean?

JESSICA. There's this voice in my head, all the time. I try to drown it out, but it's so loud. And when my heart says: 'Dear *God,* but I miss Bob Treuhaft', it says: 'Treuhaft? What sort of a name is that? You mean that little Jewish chap? Why, he looks like a door-to-door salesman. He's not like us. He doesn't pass. He talks with his hands, laughs too loud, eats too fast – '

BOB. You didn't mention my nose.

JESSICA. That too. 'He doesn't always use the right fork, or the right words, and at times there's a trace of an accent that gives him away.' And my heart says: I love everything about this man.

BOB. Wait, it does?

JESSICA. I *love* his Jewishness, I love his humour and his rightful indignation and the way he wants to repair the world. I adore it that he doesn't know what bloody fork to use, I wish to God *I* didn't! But the other voice keeps on. I've come so far, so very far, but I can hear it, all the time. And I've started to wonder, what if it isn't my sisters at all? It's me. What if it is? It must be. Some wicked, hateful part of me that thinks some human beings are superior to others, thinks I'm superior. Thinks others aren't good enough. Thinks you're not. And it's not what I believe, Bob, I loathe it and detest it, but it's in me and I can't escape. I never will.

BOB. We all have voices.

JESSICA. Not like this.

BOB. *How do you know?* You think I don't have those thoughts about you? About *your* tribe, the blood in their veins and how cold it can run? Who I might be betraying by loving you? And whether the hell it matters?

Stopped in her tracks, she stares at him.

Decca, you don't have to be the good Mitford every second of every day. You can mess up, get it wrong, act crazy as hell – you're *home.* Because all anyone needs in the world is one person to take our face in their hands and say: I choose you. I want *you.* The good and the bad, the light and the dark, I want all of you. And I always will.

JESSICA *looks to her sisters, who recede into the shadows until they are almost, if not entirely gone, for they will never entirely go.* BOB *pushes on.*

Your boss called the office last week and made me an offer straight up. I could finish up in Washington and be settled here by Christmas.

JESSICA. Is that why you came?

BOB. It's one of the reasons.

JESSICA. Could you imagine living here? It's terribly pretty, with the hills and the bay and the little narrow streets, and tremendously lively, even with blackouts and strikes –

BOB. Don't talk like the goddamn tourist board! It depends.

JESSICA. On what?

BOB. On the other reason.

He moves towards her. For once, she stands perfectly still.

JESSICA. Which is?

He takes her face in his hands. She smiles.

Business or pleasure, Mr Treuhaft?

End of play.

A Nick Hern Book

The Party Girls first published in Great Britain in 2025 as a paperback original by Nick Hern Books Limited, The Glasshouse, 49a Goldhawk Road, London W12 8QP, in association with the Marlowe Theatre, Canterbury

The Party Girls copyright © 2025 Amy Rosenthal

Amy Rosenthal has asserted her moral right to be identified as the author of this work

Cover artwork by Muse Creative

Designed and typeset by Nick Hern Books, London
Printed and bound in Great Britain by Mimeo Ltd, Huntingdon, Cambridgeshire PE29 6XX

A CIP catalogue record for this book is available from the British Library

ISBN 978 1 83904 475 5

CAUTION All rights whatsoever in this play are strictly reserved. Requests to reproduce the text in whole or in part should be addressed to the publisher. This book may not be used, in whole or in part, for the development or training of artificial intelligence technologies or systems.

Amateur Performing Rights Applications for performance, including readings and excerpts, by amateurs in the English language should be addressed to the Performing Rights Department, Nick Hern Books, The Glasshouse, 49a Goldhawk Road, London W12 8QP, *tel* +44 (0)20 8749 4953, *email* rights@nickhernbooks.co.uk, except as follows:

Australia: ORiGiN Theatrical, *tel* +61 (2) 8514 5201, *email* enquiries@originmusic.com.au, *web* www.origintheatrical.com.au

New Zealand: Play Bureau, 20 Rua Street, Mangapapa, Gisborne 4010, *tel* +64 21 258 3998, *email* info@playbureau.com

United States and Canada: Casarotto Ramsay and Associates Ltd, see details below

Professional Performing Rights Applications for performance by professionals in any medium and in any language throughout the world should be addressed to Casarotto Ramsay and Associates Ltd, *email* rights@casarotto.co.uk, www.casarotto.co.uk

No performance of any kind may be given unless a licence has been obtained. Applications should be made before rehearsals begin. Publication of this play does not necessarily indicate its availability for performance.

www.nickhernbooks.co.uk/environmental-policy

Nick Hern Books' authorised representative in the EU is
Easy Access System Europe – Mustamäe tee 50, 10621 Tallinn, Estonia
email gpsr.requests@easproject.com

www.nickhernbooks.co.uk

@nickhernbooks